TORONTO'S RAVINES
AND URBAN FORESTS

TORONTO'S RAVINES AND URBAN FORESTS

THEIR NATURAL HERITAGE AND LOCAL HISTORY

JASON RAMSAY-BROWN

JAMES LORIMER & COMPANY LTD., PUBLISHERS
TORONTO

James Lorimer & Company Ltd., Publishers acknowledges the support of the Ontario Arts Council. We acknowledge the financial support of the Government of Canada through the Canada Book Fund for our publishing activities. We acknowledge the support of the Canada Council for the Arts which last year invested $24.3 million in writing and publishing throughout Canada. We acknowledge the Government of Ontario through the Ontario Media Development Corporation's Ontario Book Initiative.

Cover design: Meredith Bangay

Library and Archives Canada Cataloguing in Publication

Ramsay-Brown, Jason, author
     Toronto's ravines and urban forests : their natural heritage and local history / Jason Ramsay-Brown.

Includes bibliographical references and index.
ISBN 978-1-4594-0875-3 (pbk.)

     1. Parks--Ontario--Toronto--Guidebooks. 2. Ravines--Ontario--Toronto--Guidebooks. 3. Urban forestry--Ontario--Toronto. 4. Trails--Ontario--Toronto--Guidebooks. 5. Toronto (Ont.)--Guidebooks. I. Title.

FC3097.65.R36 2015   333.7809713'541   C2015-900269-9

James Lorimer & Company Ltd., Publishers
317 Adelaide Street West, Suite 1002
Toronto, ON, Canada
M5V 1P9
www.lorimer.ca

Printed and bound in China

*To Abbey, whose little footsteps have led me down
so many unimaginable paths*

RAVINES & URBAN FORESTS LEGEND

1. Altona Forest
2. Rouge Park
3. Col. Danforth Park and Lower Highland Creek
4. East Point Park
5. Gates Gully
6. Warden Woods Park
7. Taylor Creek Park
8. Glen Stewart Ravine
9. L'Amoreaux North Park and Passmore Forest
10. Terraview Park and Willowfield Gardens Park
11. Charles Sauriol Conservation Reserve
12. Brookbanks Park and Deerlick Creek
13. The Leslie Street Spit and Tommy Thompson Park
14. The Forks of the Don
15. E. T. Seton Park

16. Edwards Gardens and Wilket Creek Park
17. Lower Don Recreational Trail
18. Crothers Woods and Beechwood Wetland
19. Todmorden Mills Wildflower Preserve
20. Glendon Forest
21. Moore Park Ravine and the Brick Works
22. East Don Parkland
23. Rosedale Ravine
24. Nordheimer Ravine and Glen Edyth/ Roycroft Wetlands
25. Cedarvale Ravine
26. Humber Bay Butterfly Habitat
27. King's Mill Park and Humber Marshes Park
28. Echo Valley Park
29. Etobicoke Valley Park

TORONTO

Yonge St

400

409

401

427

Bloor St

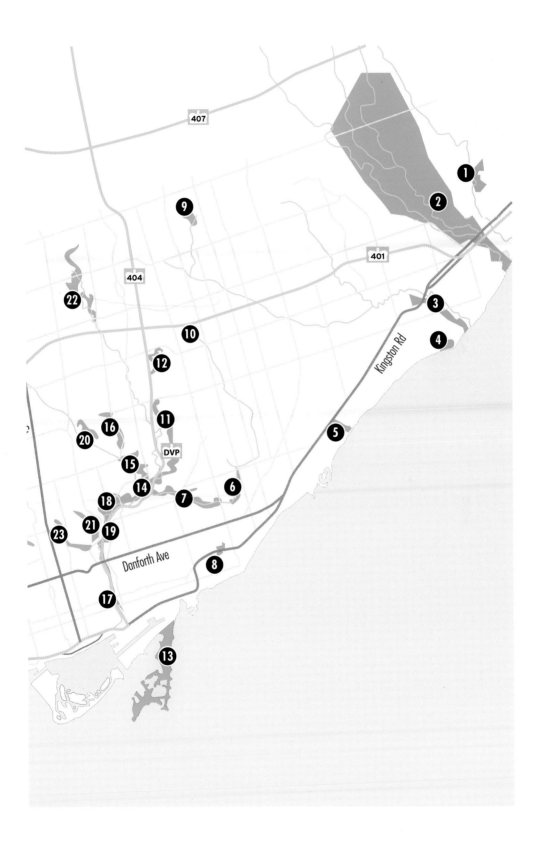

CONTENTS

INTRODUCTION

Torontonians like to think of our home as a "world-class city," in league with places like London, Paris, Tokyo, or New York. As evidence of such, we are quick to cite a robust local economy, renowned educational institutions, five-star hotels, Michelin-star restaurants, and festivals that bring in people from all around the world. Our list of successes is abundant, but these things are hardly unique to Toronto. Using them as the benchmark of our global significance serves only to set the bar as high as it has been set elsewhere, leaving ourselves the perpetual followers of others.

Of Toronto, journalist Robert Fulford once wrote:

> *Ravines are the chief characteristic of the local terrain, its topographical signature. They are both a tangible (though often hidden) part of our surroundings and a persistent force in our civic imagination. They are the shared subconscious of the municipality . . .*

The wilderness outside the window, under the bridge, down the alley, or right in our own backyard is perhaps far more the soul of the city than any of its buildings, roads, or historic landmarks. It is like the fingers of a massive, time-less hand, outstretched across the city, holding us all close. Yet, perhaps because of such subtle influence, it is too often taken for granted, absent from our civic discourse and hardly afforded a glance out the window of a rumbling subway car. Millions of Torontonians pass by, around, and over our amazing tapestry of ravines and urban forests, too busy with the challenges of day-to-day living to reflect for long upon these places as blessings, pockets of vibrant life, and histories so quintessentially Toronto.

In these greenspaces, however, things are different. Over the last several years, I've been privileged to meet hundreds of people who have succumbed to the siren call of our ravines and urban forests. They are families that play by the creeks or wander the trails on a warm summer day, commuters who have abandoned their cars to cycle to and from work along these leafy paths, stewards and conservation-ists who volunteer countless hours to restore and protect our natural heritage, or city workers who maintain the trails and facilities. Even tourists from as far afield as Italy, Iceland, Kenya, and Japan, are lured away from the galleries and museums that brought them to our city in the first place. Far more than all of the reports, essays, papers, signs, and articles I've consulted over the years, it was these people who brought life to this book. Their stories and passions unlocked the true meaning and history of these places.

Our ravines and urban forests are our greatest civic treasure. They provide us with opportunities to connect with our natural world, and with each other. They purify our waters and clean our air. They provide an aesthetic beauty that has inspired the imaginations of such renowned artists as Margaret Atwood, Doris McCarthy, Atom Egoyan, Larry Richards, Douglas Cooper, and Ernest Hemingway. They have captured and preserved the relics of human history spanning millenniums past. They define, sustain, protect, and invigorate us.

The very definition of world-class city is poised to change. One need look no further than one's own neighbourhood to observe the impact of the excesses of industrialization and consumerism. Sidewalks show trash scampering in the breeze. We have rivers too toxic to drink from, and lakes too polluted to swim in. TV and radio news programs encourage the young and elderly to seek refuge indoors on so-called "smog days." Fields and forests have fallen to strip malls and skyscrapers. In the face of these problems, it would seem obvious that the greatness of a city will no longer depend solely on the presence of a stock exchange, major league sports franchise, or vibrant nightlife. Increasingly, people are looking to cities to provide a new urban experience, one that situates the health of our natural world in balance with the opportunities provided by progress and modern convenience. From green roofs to green bins and from playgrounds to parks, the world is moving inexorably toward this new urbanity. Toronto is uniquely poised to lead the way, if only we can sustain the will to do so.

In many ways, this book is an invitation. The natural heritage and local history it provides is meant to inform and inspire, and to draw people in to these places so they can understand and experience first-hand the wonders that abound there. It is hoped that despite the potential threat of human visits, with care and caution the good outweighs the bad. Knowing these places is the first step to loving these places — and people protect what they love. If Toronto is to become the city we deserve it to be, each acre we conserve and each species we preserve is a victory now and forever.

ALTONA FOREST

1

Altona Forest can be found in the city of Pickering, right on the border of Toronto just north of Altona Rd and Sheppard Avenue. It's part of the Petticoat Creek watershed, one of the few local watersheds that does not find its source in the Oak Ridges Moraine. The creek itself skips in and out of Altona proper along its western edge, crossing through barely two hundred metres of the forest in total.

Altona is a rich and diverse place, offering a deep interior quite rare for urban forests in the Greater Toronto Area. The woods are populated by generations of sugar maple, white cedar, ironwood, white elm, and a plethora of other tree species. Spring beauty, red trillium, and endangered wood poppy bloom in the wake of the melting snow. Yellow lady's slipper and red baneberry flaunt their beauty beneath the canopy each summer. Wild rose, New England aster, and zigzag goldenrod usher in the falling leaves, which scatter themselves across the trails and forest floor in abundance. Of course, the forest is not without its invaders: buckthorn, dog-strangling vine, and garlic mustard are as plentiful here as elsewhere.

Sequestered away in Altona's south, and inaccessible to the public, lies the J. Murray Speirs Ecological Reserve, an area protected for ecological monitoring

Above: White-tailed deer
Left: Moss prospers in a stand of
dead trees

and study. This section of the forest was once the backyard of acclaimed ornithologist and professor of zoology, Dr. J. Murray Speirs, who donated the land to the Toronto and Region Conservation Authority (TRCA) in 1996. Prior to his death in 2001, Dr. Speirs had been a fixture in these woods for decades, taking walks almost every day in hopes of catching a glimpse or song of any of the over one hundred species of birds known to visit or reside in Altona.

In the north, the forest connects with the Rouge-Duffins Wildlife Corridor, a vital migration passage

Rouge-Duffins Wildlife Corridor in Altona's north

between the Rouge and Duffins valley systems. The corridor delivers an impressive array of creatures to Altona, drawn in by its copious bounty. White-tailed deer are frequently spotted on or near the forest trails. Raccoons and opossum ramble over turf amongst the thickets. Foxes scamper to and from their dens along the forest edges. Barred owls face the setting sun, on the prowl for gray tree frogs and eastern cottontail rabbits. Altona Forest is, however, perhaps best known for its pack of coyotes.

Coyotes are one of modern-day Toronto's most notable predators. Many ravines and urban forests now sport warning signs regarding this animal, advising visitors to stay on the trail, keep pets on leashes, and never, ever, to feed them. Yet a century or so ago, coyotes were not the predator that concerned us most — it was the gray wolf. Urban sprawl, coupled with our own violent persecution of the wolves, have since seen to the complete extirpation of the species from the Greater Toronto Area. In the vacancy left behind, coyotes have expanded their range and taken up residence in the city.

Above: Altona Forest wetlands
Left: Green Frog

No doubt, coyotes pose a threat to humans and to the pets we bring along with us on strolls through our local wilds. Aggressive confrontations, and even rare attacks are reported each year in the city, and are on the increase by many estimates. But it's important to realize that our ecosystems often depend on predators just like the coyote. The natural order has evolved over millennia to form a complex interplay between various species, and the extirpation of significant predators can prove detrimental to the entire system.

In recent years, white-tailed deer in Altona are beginning to have a notable impact on the site's plant community. Browsing deer have greatly reduced the population of trout lily, Canada columbine, and trillium in particular, but a whole cast of other plants have been adversely affected. As the deer whittle away the vegetation, new opportunities open for invasive plant species to take hold. In combination, loss of habitat and food sources could eventually drive some of the native wildlife from Altona. Their departure would further disrupt the local food web, leading to even more changes in the forest. Effectively, left unchecked, the

Above: Coyote
Right: Bone on the forest floor

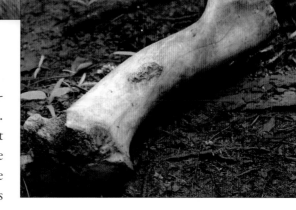

deer could very well prompt a massive change to the ecology of Altona. As much as we may worry about coyotes, we must also acknowledge that they may yet prove to be the best indigenous defense against this potential upheaval.

While coyotes are not nearly as successful at hunting deer as gray wolves are, they nonetheless do pose a specific threat to them, particularly young fawns. Equally important, the mere presence of the coyote pack may have its benefits. Where the coyotes den and hunt, other creatures both large and small naturally fear to tread. Their unwillingness to venture into these areas affords the wilds a certain protection, and provides an opportunity for rest and regrowth. Fear them as we may, it behoves us to coexist with the coyote, to find new and novel ways of ensuring human safety that do not depend on wiping them out altogether. The challenge is substantial, but if we are to take the stability and prosperity of our natural spaces seriously, it is a challenge worth facing.

ROUGE PARK

2

No discussion of Toronto's ravines and urban forests could be complete without mentioning Rouge Park. Standing as the largest nature park in all of Toronto, it provides shelter and nourishment to several hundred species of plants, hundreds of bird species, and a multitude of species of fish, mammals, amphibians, and reptiles. The park dominates roughly 13 per cent of the enormous Rouge River watershed, which constitutes about half the natural space that remains across its 33,600 hectare reach. The sanctity of the park has a direct and noted effect on the safety of drinking water in the Greater Toronto Area and on the countless lives, both human and animal, that reside in Toronto, Pickering, Markham, Richmond Hill, and Whitchurch-Stouffville.

The park helps form part of the northeastern border of the Carolinian Life Zone, one of North America's most diverse ecological regions. While this unique tapestry of forests, savannahs, wetlands, and meadows extends as far south as Tennessee, and from the Mississippi to the Appalachians, it has a minor presence in Canada. Rouge Park is not purely Carolinian, but rather a transitional zone. This, however, only serves to increase biodiversity, further contributing to the

Typical Carolinian forest (Vista Trail)

Above: Vista Trail near Twyn Rivers Drive
Left: Typical Rouge trail marker

immeasurable importance of Rouge Park as a provider of habitat and refuge to many exceedingly rare and wonderful species of plants and animals. Northern flying squirrels can be spotted gliding from branch to branch across the forest canopy. Shy bullrush, sharp-leaved goldenrod, wild blue lupine, dense blazing star, and American ginseng sprout in varied locations. Short-eared owls, least bitterns, red-shouldered hawks, and eastern loggerhead shrikes take flight throughout the park. Smoky shrews nest inside the stumps of decaying sycamore and black walnut.

While it's possible to spend many hours exploring some of Toronto's trails and wild spaces, in Rouge Park such explorations could take days. Here, a multitude of trails, both formal and informal, weave across well over four thousand hectares of landscape. Getting from one trail to another is not always easy. To fully enjoy all that the Rouge has to offer requires planning, patience, and some form of

Blazing Star

transportation to get you to and from its various discrete locations.

At the very southern edge of the park, where the Rouge River flows into Lake Ontario, is the spectacular Rouge Beach and Marsh, one of the more interesting recreational destinations in the city. Fishing enthusiasts dot the banks, trolling for northern pike, rainbow trout, pumpkinseed, brown bullhead, white perch, and black crappie. Canoes and kayaks ply the waters of the river, marsh, and lake, enjoying a unique vantage from which to watch the action in the area. Cyclists pass through along the epic Waterfront Trail, some en route to the nearby Petticoat Creek Conservation Area, others on their way towards downtown Toronto. Beach-goers splash and sun themselves on the soft sands of the lake's shore. Regardless of what brings you to this section of the Rouge, do not leave without spending some time drinking in the views of Rouge Marsh itself, one of the largest and most diverse wetlands in the Greater Toronto Area, a refuge for everything from muskrats to great blue herons.

About two kilometres north of Lake Ontario along the river lies Glen Rouge Campground, the only official campground in Toronto. Access to the site is found off Kingston Road, just north of where the Rouge River and Little Rouge Creek

Rouge Marsh

merge under the lanes of Highway 401. The campground offers over a hundred sites, including a handful accessible only to backpackers, nestled amongst the hemlock and eastern white pine that occupy much of the area. The site is also home to the southern access point for Mast Trail, one of the Rouge's more impressive routes for wandering. Running north for some two kilometres, Mast Trail leads hikers along what was once a logger's route centuries ago. The deep interior forest that surrounds this trail is virtually unique in the city, and haunted by species of birds likely found nowhere else nearby, including ovenbird, ruffed grouse, acadian flycatcher, and broad-winged hawk.

Mast Trail eventually delivers hikers to the Twyn Rivers area, a nexus of the Rouge Park trail system. Vista Trail, Orchard Trail, and Mast Trail all meander their way to Twyn Rivers Drive, providing opportunities to change trails if you are willing to walk small distances along the road itself. A parking lot services the area, located across the road from Celebration Forest, a miniscule sitting area carved out of the nearby woods. Following Twyn Rivers Drive west to its intersection with Sheppard Avenue East you'll discover Glen Eagles Vista Trail, another very short romp, but one that affords a great view of the valley in early spring and late fall.

Little Rouge Creek near Twyn Rivers Drive bridge

At the old trailhead for Orchard Trail, located in the Twyn Rivers area near the bridge that crosses Little Rouge Creek, visitors will find old stonework remaining from Maxwell's Mill, one of many mills that operated in the Rouge during the early nineteenth century. This trailhead is no longer maintained, however, and official access to Orchard Trail is now provided about one hundred metres south along Twyn Rivers Drive. The trail leads on for two or so kilometres, across land that served heavy agricultural duty in the days long ago. Apple trees can still be spotted with some ease, a testament to this fact.

Orchard Trail eventually arrives at a small pond on the southern side of Park Road, another nexus of the Rouge Park trail system. Directly across the road, a similar wetland marks the start of Cedar Trail, a two kilometre run that leads through a lovely expanse of mature forest on its way to Meadowvale Road. To the east along Park Road, visitors may note the old Beare Road landfill site, which ended a decade and a half of service in 1983. It is now home to a novel electricity production facility, which recovers methane gas from the rotting landfill and uses it to produce power. In the opposite direction along Park Road, visitors are on approach to the parking lots of the Toronto Zoo, and to the site of the Rouge

Pond on Cedar Trail by Park Road

Valley Conservation Centre (RVCC). The RVCC occupies James Pearse Jr. House, and is the typical meeting spot for many of the guided walks offered in Rouge Park.

Just south of the RVCC is Vista Trail, a gem of the local trail system. Several minutes down the trail, visitors will notice a large elevated viewing platform, compliments of Ontario Power Generation. The platform offers some of the best panoramic views to be found anywhere in Rouge Park. The trail then continues through the meadowland under the towers and lines of the hydro corridor, before dipping into the idyllic Carolinian forest that stretches from here back to Twyn Rivers Drive. Many hikers combine visits to Vista and Orchard to form a loop that takes a few hours to complete in full.

Farther to the north, segregated from the Park Road trails by agricultural fields and a railway corridor, lies Woodland Trail. Starting off of Reesor Road, just south of Steeles Avenue East, Woodland Trail largely mirrors the flow of Little Rouge River. The surrounding deciduous forest has a reputation for offering some of the best opportunities for spotting the Rouge's vibrant reptile and amphibian communities. Red eft, eastern red-backed salamanders, blue-spotted salamanders,

Blue-spotted salamander

and milksnakes are sometimes spotted in the moist leaf-litter decomposing on the forest floor. Expanses of meadowland have earned the trail a solid reputation with birders, and the surrounding area has been designated one of the city's official Bird Flyways sites.

Farther north still, Bob Hunter Memorial Park inhabits a two hundred hectare section of parkland located between Steeles Avenue East and 14th Avenue in Markham. The site is named after Robert Lorne Hunter, co-founder of Greenpeace and long-time journalist with Toronto's own CityTV and CP24. The park has been the recipient of a prestigious number of ecological remediation and renaturalization projects since it was first founded in 2006, efforts needed to help transition the area away from its largely agricultural past. Dozens of hectares of Carolinian forest and meadowland have been planted over time, and the area continues to benefit from ongoing interventions.

Opportunities for exploring and visiting Rouge Park continue to be developed year after year. In 2014, the federal government unveiled a plan to establish Rouge National Urban Park, an act which may foster even more change in the park. By adopting the existing Rouge Park from the province, and enhancing it with

Rouge Valley Conservation Centre

additional lands in federal possession, the plan proposed to provide increased ecological protection and preservation, while at the same time offering new and novel recreational opportunities for park visitors. Specific details (or lack thereof) inspired many heated debates, especially from the provincial government, who refused to pass over control of Rouge Park until ecological protections were explicitly detailed in writing by the feds. The future of one of Toronto's most precious natural spaces may remain uncertain in decades to follow, but with forethought and vigilance from environmental organizations, concerned citizens, and all levels of government, it is hoped that the discussions kindled in 2014 will give rise to a more vital and vigorous Rouge Park. The Rouge can be a jewel of urban forestry, a testament to how our natural and artificial worlds can live in harmony, inspire one another, and serve to enhance the quality of life of all living creatures who float in and between these two worlds. All we have to do is provide it with the safeguards and stewardship to do so.

COLONEL DANFORTH PARK AND LOWER HIGHLAND CREEK PARK

Wedged between the infamous flow of the Don and the impressive grandeur of the Rouge, Highland Creek is often missing from the mind maps of many Torontonians, save perhaps those who live within the heart of its watershed. Highway 401 blows past or over all four of the river's branches with no fanfare other than perfunctory river markers, and offers little more than a quick vista of treetops to impress passersby with. Arterial roads like Lawrence Avenue and Kingston Road fare much the same, leaving the creek to course in secret splendour beneath a horizon of concrete and asphalt. Despite its range and vitality, Highland Creek is almost defined by a subtlety of presence, a watercourse on the periphery of the urban experience.

During the early years of European settlement, the glacial trench of Highland Creek proved a considerable obstacle to city planners and developers. Steep grades

Highland Creek

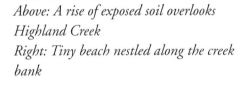

Above: A rise of exposed soil overlooks Highland Creek
Right: Tiny beach nestled along the creek bank

and sandy soil, coupled with the sheer breadth and depth of the valley itself, severely limited opportunities for road and rail crossings. While a strong and vibrant community had started to surround Highland Creek by the early nineteenth century, it was not until the 1930s that bridge-builders summoned the skill, material, and fortitude to tackle the creek valley in any meaningful way. Until then, the only way past the valley was through the valley.

An access road leads in to Colonel Danforth Park off Colonel Danforth Trail, which runs along the valley ridge and once merged with Military Trail to the east to form part of Scarborough's first highway. Following the access road to its end, you are delivered to the heart of Colonel Danforth Park and the Highland Creek Trail, which winds its way south down to Lake Ontario. The walk from

Above and left: Many mushrooms can be spotted with ease just along the trail edge

here to there is a little over two kilometres and offers some of the best opportunities to enjoy the creek anywhere in the city.

Travelling alongside Highland Creek, visitors are surrounded by outstanding forest, dominated by American beech, sugar maple, white cedar, and trembling aspen. Slippery elm and red pine, both unusual finds in Toronto, are also known to haunt these woods. While many precious plant communities thrive in Colonel Danforth Park, the area is perhaps more noteworthy for its abundance of fungi, hidden amongst the fallen logs and humus of the forest floor. Small white cup, fan-shaped jelly, mossy maple polypore, crown-tipped coral, parrot waxycap, forest funnelcap, and bleeding fairy helmet are amongst the scores and scores

30

Above: Yellow-spotted salamander
Right: Bridgework connecting Lower Highland Creek Park to the waterfront trail to Port Union

of species known to inhabit these woods.

After passing under Lawrence Avenue, Colonel Danforth Park quietly gives way to Lower Highland Creek Park, home to Stephenson's Swamp, one of the Highland Creek watershed's most important Environmentally Significant Areas and one of the city's few Provincially Significant Wetlands (PSWs). The swamp serves as breeding ground for uncommon critters like the blue-gray gnatcatcher and yellow-spotted salamander, and plays host to rare flora such as dotted wolffia and radiate sedge.

Farther south, Highland Creek Trail finally arrives at an interesting intersection of elevated trails and bridges that overlooks the mouth of Highland Creek and the driftwood-strewn shores of Lake Ontario. To the east, the Waterfront Trail passes in to Port Union. To the west, the trail delivers visitors to East Point Park, high atop the Scarborough Bluffs.

EAST POINT PARK

Perched atop the Scarborough Bluffs, south of Copperfield Road, lies a surprisingly underused bit of wild space known as East Point Park. The sixty hectare park is home to the East Point Bird Sanctuary, the first of several sites that constitute a city-wide program to preserve and enhance local bird habitat. The architecture of the sanctuary is focused around a wetland on the eastern side of the park and features a viewing pavilion, decorative bird blind, and an intriguing soundscape pavilion.

Birding has been the dominant activity at East Point Park for ages. The well-preserved meadowland and scrub here attract a spectacular assortment of breeding and migratory birds. Orchard oriole, American woodcock, Carolina wren, bufflehead, orange-crowned warbler, gray catbird, double-crested cormorant, American pipit, red-breasted merganser, pine siskin, and snow bunting are only some of hundreds of species to have been spotted in the park. Butterflies abound here too: common buckeyes, clouded sulphurs, Milbert's tortoiseshells, spring azures, pipevine swallowtails, little yellows, and hickory hairstreaks all frequent East Point Park.

The trail through the wetland eventually curves to shadow the bluffs themselves.

Above and right: Bird sanctuary bird blind and pavilion closeup

Prior to our city's visit from Hurricane Hazel, the mouth of Highland Creek could be found on the eastern edge of East Point Park underneath the bluffs. It was here, myth has it, that a ship of embattled British soldiers, squaring off against an American gunship in the War of 1812, dumped their cargo. Gold coins, copper kettles, and a variety of other treasures and curios are said to have been deposited, none of which have ever been located, despite the occasional foray by ambitious treasure hunters.

Following the trail westward are some outstanding views of Lake Ontario and of the Scarborough Bluffs themselves. On the opposite side of the trail, East Point Park displays an impressive wealth of native and non-native plant species. Staghorn sumac, Queen Anne's lace, prairie cordgrass, dame's rocket, bushy cinquefoil, Nelson's horsetail, fragrant umbrella-sedge, yarrow, feverfew, and asters all grow in delightful abundance.

Above: Trail behind bird sanctuary
Left: Downy woodpecker in staghorn sumac

The trail eventually heads northward, back to Copperfield Road, alongside the Ken Morrish Softball Complex. Circling around to the eastern side of the site via Copperfield Road is a dangerous proposition, so most visitors opt to double-back along the trail. Other small trails do exist that weave into the park's interior, but the views of the lake and bluffs are simply too wonderful for many to resist.

GATES GULLY

Ten-thousand-year-old archaeological artifacts, a passageway for smugglers, a secret stash of British treasure, and a sanctuary for artists, Gates Gully (Bellamy Ravine) is a unique and magnificent part of Toronto's urban wilderness and its local history. It is a place full of legends, legacy, and beauty. The ravine cleaves through the Scarborough Bluffs down to Lake Ontario from the intersection of Bellamy Road and Kingston Road, dropping about ninety metres in elevation over its one-kilometre length. As one of the few places along the bluffs that affords convenient access between the lake and the flats above, it is an area that has been visited and inhabited by humans for at least ten thousand years, likely much longer. Relics unearthed here by Ashley and Harold McCowan have been reliably dated from the early Archaic period (ca. 8,000 BCE).

When European settlers began to occupy these lands at the end of the eighteenth century, Gates Gully continued to serve as a major access route down to the waters of Lake Ontario. Likely because of this, what is now the intersection of Bellamy and Kingston quickly became an important epicentre of community in the region and home to a very popular inn and tavern built by Jonathan Gates.

Deciduous forest along Doris McCarthy Trail, alongside Bellamy Ravine Creek

This tavern's most notable claim to fame is that on the night of December 5, 1837, it served as a rallying point for the first township militia that had arrived to defend Toronto against the erupting threat of William Lyon Mackenzie and his rebels. These men, under the command of Colonel Archibald MacLean, marched on to join the forces of Colonel Allan MacNab and were amongst the artillery fire in the Battle of Montgomery's Tavern on December 7, 1837, effectively the start of the Upper Canada Rebellion. It was in honour of Jonathan Gates and his tavern that Bellamy Ravine was christened Gates Gully in 1993.

The soldiers and merchants who plied the waters of Lake Ontario found Gates Gully an alluring destination. The ability to covertly haul up cargo sent from American ports was an attractive and elusive opportunity, and smugglers of contraband goods and equipment made good use of it. Gates Gully offered a great lookout from atop the Bluffs, a convenient beach for small craft landings, and a gentle enough incline to make it possible to wheel up cargo by wagon — a sort of smuggler's trifecta. During the late 1830s, when smuggling experienced a bit of a heyday as folks were looking to avoid a dreaded import tax of one pound and three pence, the ravine was used regularly to bring in an assortment of merchandise including tea, tobacco, and leather.

Doris McCarthy trail about a half a kilometre from trail head

While the military may not have used the ravine in the same way local smugglers did, a few soldiers found refuge there over the decades. During a meeting of the York Pioneers Historical Society in November, 1931, Levi E. Annis (once assistant commissioner for the Dominion in Great Britain) told one of the more intriguing stories about the area. The Annis family were amongst the first non-native Canadians to live in the Bluffs area, and, at the dawn of the nineteenth century, were pivotal in blazing a trail that would eventually become Kingston Road. Their reputation was known far and wide, so much so that rebel leader William Lyon Mackenzie was said to have hidden out at their homestead sometime in 1837, while evading government forces. The story Levi told, passed down through his family, claims that as the Americans burned and looted the fledgling city during the Battle of York, in April 1813, British soldiers staying with the Annis family made their way to Gates Gully and buried all of the money they had on hand. No one knew just how much this was exactly, but clearly enough to be worth the effort of burying. Apparently, Levi claimed, the treasure was never recovered by the soldiers, nor by any treasure hunter, himself included, who went in search of it in the years that followed.

Today, of course, the public trail that leads to the lake serves purely recreational

View of Lake Ontario from Doris McCarthy Trail

Outflow of Bellamy Ravine Creek into Lake Ontario

ends, providing visitors with a path through the heart of nearly twenty-four hectares of ravine land. Dubbed the Doris McCarthy Trail, after the renowned Canadian artist, in 2001, it more or less shadows Bellamy Ravine Creek, a combined engineered drainage channel and natural waterway that runs along the bottom of the ravine. The steep surrounding slopes play host to a primarily deciduous forest, and native species like white and yellow birch, American beech, white oak, and sugar maple can be spotted with ease. The eastern slopes are reputed to be more aggressively disturbed than their western counterparts, the understory teaming with the usual cast of invasives found in Toronto, including dog-strangling vine, garlic mustard, and buckthorn. But the ravine is also home to a variety of region-ally rare plant species, most notably blue cohosh, downy ryegrass, thin-leaved sunflower, russet buffaloberry, and Hitchcock's sedge.

Wandering along the trail, it's not at all uncommon to observe some of the amazing wildlife that haunts so much of Toronto's urban forest. Deer, beaver, foxes, and coyotes are reported here several times a season. Listen carefully and you're sure to hear the antics of some eastern chipmunks or the chatter of a red-winged blackbird. Peek between the rocks and sedges, and you may just find an eastern garter snake or eastern red-backed salamander. Watch the wildflowers and catch glimpses of visiting butterflies like the wild indigo duskywing, cabbage white, red admiral, and spring azure.

Warbler

Like many of the natural areas along the Toronto shoreline, Gates Gully is a significant stopover for migratory birds and serves as valuable hunting and nesting grounds for our own domestic populations. Over one hundred different species have been spotted and identified in and around Gates Gully, including a variety of grebes, warblers, herons, ducks, kinglets, mergansers, hawks, gulls, woodpeckers, and terns. Large colonies of bank swallows are known to nest just east of the ravine, along the bluffs.

Where the Doris McCarthy Trail opens up to the shores of Lake Ontario, you are immediately confronted by the imposing visage of Marlene Hilton Moore's outdoor sculpture, *Passage*. According to the artist, "The form of this Cor-Ten steel sculpture is based upon the ribcage of the fish and the ribs of the canoe. *Passage* links together the idea of a significant passage through life, the passage of the fish through the water that shapes this site, and the silent passage of the canoe, symbol of the exploration of our land. The interior base simulates an architectural scale ruler whose stylized end resembles the trillium, provincial flower of Ontario." Installed in 2002, the sculpture is meant to honour artist Doris McCarthy and the Scarborough Bluffs themselves.

The connection between Doris McCarthy and Gates Gully begins in 1939, when a twenty-nine-year-old McCarthy purchased a parcel of land atop the bluffs on the western side of the ravine. Her mother considered the purchase extravagant

Passage, *by Marlene Hilton Moore*

and referred to it as "that fool's paradise of yours." Once owned by the McCowan family (after whom nearby McCowan Avenue is named), the twelve-acre property was purchased with only a small one-room cottage on it. By the winter of 1940, with the help of architect Forest Telfer, McCarthy had started extensive renovations on the place, constructing a residence she would come to call "Fool's Paradise." She spent her remaining years living here, occasionally opening it up as an artist's refuge and retreat to the likes of singer-songwriter Lorraine Segato. Until recently, the site was off limits to visitors save for about three days in the last few years (during Doors Open Toronto).

McCarthy lived in Fool's Paradise until her death on November 25, 2010, but spent the better part of the two decades prior preparing a legacy for the land. In 1986, McCarthy donated seven acres to the Toronto and Region Conservation Authority (TRCA) in recognition of its geological and ecological significance. In 1998, the remaining acreage and homestead were bequeathed to the Ontario Heritage Trust with the understanding that it would be preserved and used as a retreat for future artists to enjoy.

McCarthy's donation of land to the TRCA came at a time when the impact of

Scarborough Bluffs just west of ravine, the approximate location of Fool's Paradise property

erosion on the Scarborough Bluffs was solidifying as a hot-button issue in municipal planning and politics. While some locals may take them for granted, the bluffs are, in fact, one of the geological marvels of North America. Noted geologist A. P. Coleman, whose work essentially redefined the study of ice age climatology, once said, "The history of the last million years has been more completely recorded in the deposits in [the bluffs] than anywhere else in Canada or perhaps the world." Their preservation is not only imperative to residents of the local community, but to members of the international scientific community, who still have much to learn from these amazing natural features. Sadly, despite McCarthy's generosity, the area surrounding Gates Gully remained one of the least-protected sectors of the bluffs for almost two decades.

Ongoing erosion control efforts have reformed the shoreline here in a fashion very reminiscent of the Leslie Street Spit and Tommy Thompson Park. Construction rubble and beach cobble have been used to craft a variety of headlands and breakwaters, creating a strip of land that, while clearly artificial, is not without its own charming aesthetic. Certain never to be a destination for volleyball or sun tanning, there is little doubt it will do an outstanding job at helping to preserve this precious and important natural area.

WARDEN WOODS PARK

6

As the last ice age was ending some 13,000 years ago, much of Warden Woods Park was a part of the shoreline of Glacial Lake Iroquois, the prehistoric lake that later became Lake Ontario. This enormous lake, with a water level about thirty metres higher than the present-day lake, existed because the great Laurentide Ice Sheet was acting as a province-sized dam, blocking the rivers of the Saint Lawrence valley. Without this traditional drainage route, the waters of Glacial Lake Iroquois backed up until relief was provided by the Mohawk River valley, eventually draining into what we now call the Hudson River.

Back then, the mouth of Taylor-Massey Creek breached a small bay that lay sheltered behind a huge sand spit, a predecessor of today's Toronto Islands. This spit provides a bit of geological foreshadowing of one of the major problems endured by Warden Woods: erosion on a monumental scale. Taylor-Massey Creek is possibly the most urbanized waterway in Toronto. It begins near Terraview Park and Willowfield Gardens Park as stormwater collected from sixteen hectares of Highway 401. The creek is then fed by scores of additional storm sewers and watercourses as it winds its way down to Warden Woods, predominantly via a

Outflow of Taylor Creek into Warden Woods under St. Clair

man-made concrete channel. The end result is that stormwater from uncountable kilometres of roadway is dumped directly into the creek. The resulting flash floods essentially tear through Warden Woods on their way towards the East Don River down by the Forks, scouring the natural creek bed with great violence as they go.

The ravine's sandy soil has been ravaged over the decades, particularly in the northern end of the park by St. Clair Avenue. The damage throughout has been so severe that sections of trail have been relocated to ensure public safety. Trees are routinely felled when their exposed root systems are deemed insufficient to the task of holding them upright much longer, and new plantings are attended to in hopes of providing for future defence. Armour stone has been installed in various highly susceptible areas to help stabilize the creek banks, and ongoing monitoring will no doubt inspire similar such installations in the years to come. All combined, these efforts have slowed down the damage being wrought, but we're still a long way from where we need to be.

Unfortunately, stormwater is not the only thing that makes its way into Taylor-Massey Creek. Thanks to the presence of combined sewer overflows (CSO) and

Armour stone along the creek

illegal residential sewage hookups, the water quality in Warden Woods has been a hot-button issue since the turn of the millennium. A 2002–03 study conducted by Lake Ontario Waterkeeper discovered that the most contaminated discharge was found in Toronto's Warden Woods, where E. coli levels were "two thousand times higher than provincial water quality objectives." Remediation efforts continue, but it's a complex problem that stretches far outside the borders of Warden Woods Park. Taylor-Massey Creek requires the kind of change that is much greater than environmental groups and the city can muster alone. Remediation of the creek depends on the participation of the innumerable residents and commercial interests that line its course from end to end, and gaining this participation has proven to be far more difficult than one might have hoped.

Warden Woods is a special, vital place. Much of the lands were acquired by the township of Scarborough in 1959 from the Sisters of St. Joseph, a Catholic order that had begun its humanitarian efforts in the area over a century beforehand. Ownership by the Sisters largely protected the area from much of the more grievous assaults wrought by construction and development in the surrounding area. As a result, Warden Woods is home to many stands of mature growth forest, including fine specimens of sugar maple, American beech, and red oak, some over a century old. It supports a fantastic diversity of plant life, ranging from common species like cattail and pussy willow, to more unusual ones such as downy arrowwood, false dragonhead, Canada wild lettuce, rose twisted stalk, and white bear

Butternut tree

sedge. According to the city, roughly three hundred unique plant species have been catalogued across the thirty-five hectares of Warden Woods, an accomplished inventory for a park of this size.

Warden Woods is also home to some increasingly scarce butternut trees in Toronto. The butternut is currently protected under Ontario's *Endangered Species Act* due to a serious fungal disease called butternut canker, first identified in Ontario in 1991. Butternut canker can destroy a tree in only a few years, and roughly one-third of the Ontario butternut population was wiped out over the first two decades following its emergence. So dire is their plight that the Ontario Forest Gene Conservation Association has been compelled to institute a program to propagate seedlings from disease-resistant trees in hopes of repopulating native areas. The butternuts in Warden Woods are unlikely to be resistant to the canker, and it is altogether possible their days in the park could be numbered.

The great diversity of flora in Warden Woods, coupled with its intentional absence of artificial lighting, make it an important habitat for a wealth of local and migratory birds. Sharp-shinned hawks and American crows cruise the skies above in search of prey. Belted kingfishers and green heron patrol the creek. The knocks

Above: Gus Harris Trail
Right: Robin on staghorn

of downy and hairy woodpeckers sound from around the bend. Sparrows, robins, vireos, kinglets, and warblers flit and flap from bush to tree.

As a visitor to Warden Woods Park, the best way you can help to preserve the integrity of this fragile environment is to stick to the main paved path, dubbed the Gus Harris Trail. (Christened on June 1, 2002, the trail honours Augustus John Harris, a career politician who had served in a variety of roles, including as reeve of Scarborough Township in 1956 and eventually as Scarborough's mayor from 1979–88.) Staying on the path is the only way to ensure your footfalls do not damage rare plant life or threaten the constitution of the landscape. Further, it is the only way through the park that guarantees your safety. While the western side of the park is filled with tiny side trails, at least one of them passes the sandy edge of Warden Woods' highest bluff, which offers absolutely no barriers to protect hikers from stumbling over its crumbling edge.

TAYLOR CREEK PARK

7

Taylor Creek Park, an enormous natural area covering hundreds of hectares, follows the course of Taylor-Massey Creek from Victoria Park Avenue west to the Forks of the Don. This creek is one of the most significant tributaries of the Don River in the city, so much so that what we know today as the East Don River was originally called the Middle Don, and Taylor-Massey Creek was referred to as the East Don.

Taylor-Massey Creek is a very polluted waterway, one of the worst in the city by all accounts. In *Forty Steps to a New Don*, a watershed plan issued in 1994 by the Toronto and Region Conservation Authority (TRCA), Taylor-Massey Creek was described as holding "the dubious honour of being the most degraded of the main tributaries of the Don watershed. Its middle to upper reaches are barely recognizable as a river, having been piped or channelized in concrete. Throughout its length, storm sewers carry millions of gallons of untreated storm drainage into its waters. Heavy rain may cause sanitary sewage and even industrial discharges to flow into the creek through combined sewer overflows (CSOs)."

Since 1994, tens of millions of dollars and countless hours of labour have been

Approach to the wetland

poured into various efforts to revitalize Taylor-Massey Creek. The city, organizations like Friends of the Don East and the Taylor-Massey Project, and members of the local community have all taken an active hand in seeking to improve this troubled watercourse and the habitat that surrounds it. Trees have been planted, illegal sewer hookups have been shut down, city infrastructure has been modified, and tons of garbage and contaminated soils have been removed. Sadly, in recovering from mistakes as grievous as those inflicted upon this area over the past century or two, all this only amounts to a valiant start.

Perhaps the most ambitious of these naturalization projects happened right at the park's easternmost border, just off Victoria Park Avenue: the Taylor Creek Park Wetland. The Metro Toronto and Region Conservation Authority (MTRCA) secured these lands in 1959, but did very little other than allow them to fall victim to massive degradation in the following decades. In the 1990s, conservationists and nearby residents began an increasingly fervent discussion about how to rescue the area from its dystopian fate. This gave birth to the idea of transforming the wet, junk-riddled meadows between Dawes Road and Victoria Park Avenue into a wetland.

Taylor Creek wetland

The value of wetlands cannot be overstated. These complex and biologically diverse habitats are responsible for a wealth of ecological functions that have a direct impact not only on our natural world, but even on our most urban environments. Wetlands soak up rainfall and runoff and release them slowly over time, offering substantial storm protection and flood control. These waters are purified in the wetlands, as excess nutrients are extracted, pollutants are filtered, harmful bacteria are neutralized, and toxic sediments settle. The purified water improves groundwater recharge and stream-flow maintenance. On top of all this, the wetland serves as vital habitat to a staggering number of species, offering them sustenance and protection, and strengthening links in the local food web.

Despite these benefits, the Taylor Creek Park Wetland project was preceded by much controversy. Many people doubted the sustainable logistics of cultivating and managing a wetland here. Some argued that the funds and labour required for a project of this scale would be much better applied elsewhere. Some felt the project went too far, while others felt that it didn't go far enough. There were even

Above: Bloodroot
Right: Female mallard in Taylor Creek wetlands

those who argued that the area was already beyond hope and that efforts to reclaim it were an act of futility. In the end, the project went forward, and the site celebrated its official opening on June 12, 2009, after about a year and a half of construction.

A small, semicircular path leads off from the park's main trail to a quaint little lookout affording views into the heart of the wetland. The area supports some magnificent plant life: nannyberry, black elderberry, meadowsweet, chokecherry, snowdrops, and bloodroot all take root in and around the pond. Such plants offer a figurative banquet for native wildlife, and on any given day, you should not be surprised to find green frogs, leopard frogs, American toads, painted and snapping turtles, mallard ducks, great blue herons, and red-tailed hawks enjoying what the wetland has to offer. Cattail, a favoured material for muskrat lodges, grows here in abundance, and visitors quite often catch glimpses of these creatures mucking about the northern side of the water, playful against a backdrop of black walnut,

Ferris Tributary

yellow birch, eastern white pine, and what are said to be some of the oldest oaks along the entirety of Taylor-Massey Creek.

Wetlands aside, the run of Taylor-Massey Creek between Victoria Park Avenue and Dawes Road is also of historic interest. In the late nineteenth century, one hundred hectares of the surrounding area was purchased for use as a hobby farm by Walter Massey, president of the Massey-Harris Company and the philanthropist behind Massey Hall. The farm, known as Dentonia Park, produced eggs, poultry, and trout, but was most famous for its dairy. Massey's City Dairy Company was the first to introduce pasteurized milk to Canada. Pasteurization destroys harmful bacteria that can be present in milk and was credited for greatly reducing diseases like tuberculosis, scarlet fever, and typhoid fever in and around Toronto. Sadly, however, Walter Massey himself contracted typhoid fever and passed away in 1901, leaving his wife, Susan Marie Denton, to oversee the operation of the farm. In the decades that followed, Susan parcelled off pieces of land and donated them to the city. After her death in 1938, much of the remaining lands became the property of the borough of East York. The last surviving structure from the days of

Goulding Estate, now home to the Children's Peace Theatre

the Massey family farm, the Goulding Estate, remains on the northern perimeter of the park, just east of Dawes Road, and was declared a heritage site in 1995.

The main trail through Taylor Creek Park eventually dips under a bridge on Dawes Road. On the other side of a small parking lot, the paved path continues along the southern creek bank with few notable features other than the occasional recreational area and the beauty of the ravine itself. Peeking out from the nearby bush, one can easily spot natives like staghorn sumac, fragrant sumac, hemlock, witch hazel, and beaked hazel, as well as alien species like crack willow, weeping willow, and lilac.

A little over a kilometre west of Dawes Road, near the exit to Stan Wadlow Park, observant visitors may note a small watercourse that joins Taylor-Massey Creek from the north. This is the Ferris Tributary, which flows into Taylor Creek Park from its modern-day headwaters near Cedarcrest Boulevard. Ferris Ravine is considered part of Taylor Creek Park's official Environmentally Significant Area (ESA), a designation awarded to a large section of the surrounding wilds due to sightings of regionally rare plants and animals, including white oak, sweet fern, and the elusive star-nosed mole.

Taylor Creek public fire pit, one of the few left in Toronto's parks system

Farther west along the path, the next significant landmark is Woodbine Bridge, which carries traffic over the ravine along O'Connor Drive. Colloquially, most folks call it the O'Connor Bridge but, constructed in 1932, the bridge actually predates that road. O'Connor Drive itself was formalized afterward, with significant assistance from Frank Patrick O'Connor, the founder of Laura Secord Chocolates and senatorial representative for Scarborough Junction. Back in 1932, the bridge was effectively an extension of Woodbine Avenue, built to increase access to communities along Victoria Park Avenue and to foster continued development of the area in between. To this end, early East York people-mover Hollinger Bus Lines, which operated from the corner of Woodbine Avenue and Plains Road, soon made use of the bridge to expand its operations to the east, greatly fuelling the growth of the Parkview Hills, Woodbine Gardens, and Topham Park neighbourhoods.

Passing under the bridge, you're entering what used to be the estate lands of the Taylor family, which extended all the way to Broadview Avenue and throughout the Don Valley. The Taylor brothers operated various mills, formed the Don Valley Brick Works, and were amongst the more prominent families in nineteenth century Toronto. Their legacy is now honoured, along with that of the Massey family, by the creek that bears their name.

Two footbridges west of Woodbine Bridge, the trail passes over the Curity

Footbridge over Curity Tributary

Tributary. These waters flow out of the Curity Ravine, an isolated track of urban wilds that extend from here northeast to Curity Avenue, roughly paralleling O'Connor Drive. Despite the earth trails that head into this parcel of land, exploration of the area is strongly discouraged. Curity Ravine has been noted as one of the more pristine wildlife habitats to be found in the city and is home to significant and sensitive wetlands. There are far too few places like Curity left in Toronto, and the isolation it enjoys should be protected from our own curiosity as much as it is from the ravages of urban development.

The remainder of the Taylor Creek Park path winds through quintessential Toronto ravine on its way to the Forks of the Don. Buttercups, milkweed, goldenrod, and asters sprout up along the trail's edge. Moist and shady slopes are home to beech, birch, and maples that tower over flowering raspberry, jack-in-the-pulpit, and bluebead lily. Red-winged blackbirds, cedar waxwings, indigo buntings, goldfinches and kinglets swoop and sing in the skies above. But it is also this section of the ravine that is known to serve as occasional host to one of Toronto's most violent invasive plants: giant hogweed.

Giant hogweed looks, to the untrained eye, surprisingly similar to a variety of related plants such as cow parsnip, common hogweed, and to a lesser extent, some

City warning that giant hogweed may be nearby

types of angelica. It is most easily distinguished from these other plants by its height, which can range from two to seven metres. Of course, such height comes with age, which can leave a bit of ambiguity in the intervening time. Unlike these other plants, however, the clear sap of this noxious weed can cause severe blisters and burns, some of which can produce scars that remain even years later. Should the sap make contact with your eyes, it can lead to temporary or even permanent blindness. Technically, the plant is phototoxic, meaning these reactions only occur after exposure to light, but for obvious reasons, this is hardly a comfort. The city takes giant hogweed extremely seriously, and will secure the site of such plants with yellow caution tape and/or signage until proper removal and disposal. Regardless, given the severity of a potential encounter with the plant, visitors to Taylor Creek Park are wisely advised to learn what giant hogweed looks like, and stay clear of any plant that appears similar, particularly any which sport umbrella-shaped flowerheads dotted with tiny white flowers.

GLEN STEWART RAVINE

8

Clambering down the steep, twisting staircase that connects Kingston Road to the floor of Glen Stewart Ravine, you immediately know you're somewhere special. Glen Stewart is dominated by red oak, and in fact supports one of the largest collections in the city. Amazing specimens can be spotted with ease, clustering on the slopes, flanking water-filled depressions, towering beside the trail. Saplings rise at the feet of mature specimens, some more than thirty metres tall. So important is this inventory that the city's Tree Seed Diversity Project collected acorns here in hopes of enhancing genetic diversity elsewhere in Toronto.

The amazing red oaks at Glen Stewart are hardly its only claim to fame. First designated as an Environmentally Significant Area (ESA) in 1982, the ravine is also home to many regionally rare plant species. Fly honeysuckle, sassafras, trailing arbutus, running strawberry-bush, interrupted fern, and bluebead lily have all been catalogued here. These precious species lie nestled alongside an abundance of other interesting species like Canada honewort, early meadowrue, two-leaf toothwort, and large-flowered bellwort.

The eleven hectare ravine is home to Ames Creek, a tiny, spring-fed waterway

Giant red oak

Above: Red oak and acorns
Right: Ames Creek

that flows across the valley. In 1872, Anglican minister William Stewart Darling bought much of the ravine and surrounding land, building his home, Glen Stewart, at what is now 6 Benlamond Drive. The ravine, which was then known as Ben Lamond Park, was used by locals as a recreational area with Darling's permission. In the 1920s, investment dealer Alfred Ernest Ames built one of Toronto's first golf courses just west of the ravine, hence the name Ames Creek.

While the Beach community blossomed around it, this small tract of ravine managed to endure

Elevated boardwalk

because of its value as a neighbourhood refuge. *Endure* is the operative word —
over the decades, locals have almost loved this ravine to death, or at least to significant degredation. The ravine has been carved up by impromptu trails, eroded by
off-trail adventures, and threatened by years of abuse and misuse. To add to this
onslaught, the city included Glen Stewart as part of its twelve Discovery Walks
and designated it an interpretive trail for use by school groups excited to learn
more about Toronto's ravine system. This has drawn in visitors from all across the
city, amplifying the stress and strain Glen Stewart is subjected to.

The forest stood strong despite this, but the city came to question how long
it might be able to do so. Planning started in 2008 has since inspired a number
of rehabilitation efforts in the ravine. Elevated boardwalks, equipped with waist-
high fencing, work to forcibly restrain some of Glen Stewart's more enthusiastic
guests. Protection fencing three-beams high and backed by chicken wire has been
installed throughout. New staircases have been built in hopes of reducing the
allure of informal access points and to ensure public safety. So long as visitors learn
to respect these new additions to the ravine, Glen Stewart will have a much needed
chance to heal, something that will benefit everyone who loves this amazing bit of
our city's green space.

L'AMOREAUX NORTH PARK AND PASSMORE FOREST

L'Amoreaux North Park, named after eighteenth century Huguenot settler Josue L'Amoreaux, is located on the north side of McNicoll Avenue between Birchmount and Kennedy Roads. The park is home to two very important ecological features: L'Amoreaux Pond, which occupies much of the southeast corner of the site, and Passmore Forest, a small woodlot that rises up in the northwest corner of the property. Together, these features hearken back to the Ontario of centuries past, a history that too easily could have been lost to us, swallowed by the city's ceaseless growth.

Following the path that encircles L'Amoreaux Pond to its northern end, visitors will discover a pair of Heritage Toronto plaques that were first installed here in 2008. The plaques provide a very brief description of the Alexandra Site, an important and impressive archaeological site unearthed nearby at the turn of the

West Highland Creek outflow into L'Amoreaux North Park

century. In 2000, a planned housing development was beginning preparatory work just north of L'Amoreaux Park. When ceramic sherds were discovered but a few dozen centimetres under the surface of a farmer's field, a full-scale archaeological assessment quickly revealed a site of some significance. Eight months of excavation and analysis unearthed a 2.6 hectare Huron-Wendat village, estimated to have been built during the Middle Iroquoian period, ca. 1350.

While far from the largest or most vital village in the Huron-Wendat confederacy, it appears to have supported sixteen longhouses, three middens (basically garbage pits), and numerous auxiliary features like sweat lodges and hearths. Archaeologists suggest the village would likely have supported a population of eight hundred to a thousand people. Interestingly, given the four or five decades the village was thought to have been occupied, the Alexandra Site shows no evidence of palisades, the large fortified fences often built around such villages to protect them from invasion and attack. This suggests the village must not have found itself under threat from raids or warfare with any regularity, which would have been somewhat unusual for the times.

Remarkably, over 19,000 artifacts were recovered during excavation of the site. These included a variety of stone tools and weapons, rolled copper beads, worked bone, animal remains, and an impressive number of ceramic vessels, pipes, and sherds. Perhaps the most significant discovery, however, were beads made from

West Highland Creek flowing into L'Amoreaux Pond

seashells believed to have originated in the Atlantic Ocean. Finding beads like these several hundred kilometres from the eastern seaboard clearly demonstrates the incredible trading network the First Nations people enjoyed at the time.

Were it not for the increasingly strict legislation governing archaeological conservation that has evolved over the last few decades, there is absolutely no question that treasures like the Alexandra Site would have fallen to the march of profit and progress with barely a whimper. Archaeological Services Inc., the company responsible for the bulk of the excavation work at the Alexandra Site, suggests that approximately eight thousand archaeological heritage sites were destroyed in the Greater Toronto Area between 1951 and 1991 alone. While land developers may have occasion to bemoan the burdens and hurdles put upon them by all levels of government, the rest of us should be most grateful. The cultural heritage uncovered in places like the Alexandra Site benefits not only all Canadians, but people the world over. Each discovery, however minor, deepens our understanding and appreciation of human history and connects us with a story we can learn about in almost no other way.

Less than fifty metres northwest of the Heritage Toronto plaques, a small bridge crosses over West Highland Creek, the waterway responsible for feeding L'Amoreaux Pond. As the name implies, this creek is a tributary of Highland Creek proper and is part of what has been labelled one of the most highly developed

A red trillium growing amongst white trillium on the forest floor

watersheds in the Greater Toronto Area. The bridge hovers above an artificial catchment that often demonstrates what this development means in real terms. While the headwaters of West Highland Creek are found just north of L'Amoreaux Park, on any given day, the catchment is quite likely to be littered with refuse, bits of plastic, oil slicks, and other similar telltale signs of the creek's short journey through suburbia en route to L'Amoreaux Pond. Ecologically, the pond does help to filter and improve the quality of the these waters, but what flows out of the pond and under McNicoll Avenue still has much more to endure on its way down to join Highland Creek in Morningside Park.

On the other side of West Highland Creek a fork in the path leads visitors up a short incline to the shady bliss of Passmore Forest. The forest is named after F. F. Passmore, the surveyor responsible for Scarborough's first official maps. Scarborough Council commissioned an inaugural survey in 1850 and a second in 1862 in order to resolve several land claim disputes. His finished product, delivered by 1864, shows Scarborough in its infancy — a tapestry of private farms connected by roughly one hundred and twenty-five side roads. While this is a far cry from the amalgamated megalopolis of today, these surveys do hint at the future that lay waiting. Forest cover in Scarborough is estimated to have dropped by almost 40 per cent between the two surveys, thanks to the agricultural efforts of the swelling population and the commercial activities of roughly fifteen mills operating in the area by the

*Above: Section of Passmore Forest Trail being
colonized by invasive burdock*
Right: Eastern white pines

early 1860s. Today, F. F. Passmore's namesake forest remains one of the last stands of old growth in the area.

Passmore may only be a tiny tableland woodlot, but entering it feels more like stepping in to one of our provincial parks than your typical urban forest or ravine. The trails that criss-cross Passmore lead through a diversely populated mixed forest, peppered by mature stands of sugar maple, patches of American beech, and fine examples of white pine and red oak. Scattered throughout are numerous trees literally hollowed out by decay and the activities of creatures like pileated woodpeckers and wood-boring insects. The vibrant and varied understory teams with flowering raspberry, fairy spud, white and red trillium, wild grape, trout lily, and multiple species of fern. Like all Toronto's wild spaces, Passmore is home to its fair share of invasive species as well. The trail edge sports some of the most outrageous patches of burdock you may ever see, and all along you'll find salsify (goat's beard) whose massive dandelion-like

L'Amoreaux Pond

blowballs can be seen swaying in the breeze from afar.

Passmore offers roughly one and a half kilometres of interior trails to walk. That said, all of these trails intersect one another, allowing visitors to impulsively loop back along various sections of trail to extend their stroll as long as they desire. And a lovely stroll it is. Beams of sunlight readily breach the canopy, flashing off the fluttering leaves of the trembling aspen. Foxes, skunks, raccoons, squirrels, and chipmunks can be found (or at least heard) scampering through the woods en route from pond to den or nest. Blue jays and brown-headed cowbirds flit from tree to tree on the hunt for food. It's a place that's easy to feel lost in, if only lost in thought.

To the south, the woodlot narrows to a point, framed by a nexus of paved paths that drive foot traffic between L'Amoreaux Pond, L'Amoreaux Park, and the neighbouring community. Small, well-developed foot trails can be found throughout this area, which leads down to the pond. At the water's edge, you may find benches nestled in the bush, offering idyllic views over this important habitat. Canada geese drift across the water, calling out to one another in chorus. Garter snakes roam the grasses, while common whitetail dragonflies dart from shrub to shrub. Blue-ringed dancer damselflies attempt to mate while narrowly avoiding being gobbled up by the small fish that call the pond home. Great blue heron hunt the fish in turn, perched atop downed tree branches that break the surface of the pond. It's a wonderful place to sit, rest awhile, and extend your stay in this amazing piece of Toronto's urban wilds.

10

TERRAVIEW PARK AND WILLOWFIELD GARDENS PARK

Terraview Park and Willowfield Gardens Park are adjacent to one another, straddling Penworth Road barely a few hundred metres from the intersection of Highway 401 and Pharmacy Avenue. Looking at a map, one could easily assume these parks to be your run-of-the-mill Toronto recreational green spaces, sporting a splash pad, sports field, and a well-maintained little playground equipped with the usual slides and swings. What these sources fail to indicate, however, is that Terraview Park and Willowfield Gardens Park (often referred to as Terraview-Willowfield) also represent one of the most outstanding success stories in Toronto's renaturalization efforts.

In the 1950s, the headwaters of Taylor-Massey Creek could be found near Sheppard and Victoria Park Avenues, and the waters flowed down through Terraview-Willowfield. During the most aggressive construction period of

Overlooking Terraview Pond from the highest point in park

Highway 401, the headwaters were diverted over to Highland Creek in order to minimize engineering complications for the new Toronto Bypass, as it was then called. Taylor-Massey Creek soon found itself burdened with new headwaters: stormwater collected from sixteen hectares of what has since become one of the busiest highways in North America. This stormwater, and the inconceivable volumes of cigarette butts, motor oil, consumer garbage, road salt, industrial pollutants, and residential pesticides, were then channelled into a barren concrete ditch that crossed Terraview Park and Willowfield Gardens Park on its way to the nearby Hydro corridor and on farther south towards Warden Woods.

Over the decades, the effects were nothing short of devastating. The 1990s watershed plan *Forty Steps to a New Don* noted that Terraview-Willowfield exhibited extensive problems in terms of water quality and quantity, aquatic and terrestrial habitat, and general watershed management practices. Andrew B. Anderson of Schollen & Company, Inc., who assisted with eventual renaturalization efforts, described the original site as "sterile and uninspiring" and "little more than wide open expanses of pesticide-laden grass bisected by an open concrete storm sewer and abutted by a major highway." Voices from the local community echoed these sentiments, usually with much greater disdain. The effects on Taylor-Massey Creek and the Don River watershed were utterly nightmarish.

By the beginning of the twenty-first century, Terraview-Willowfield had become a focal point for Toronto's environmental restoration movement. Hundreds of

Terraview Pond on a clear day

participants tackled research and renaturalization efforts, including the students of Terraview-Willowfield Public School, volunteers with organizations like Friends of the Don East, staff at the Toronto and Region Conservation Authority (TRCA) and Schollen & Company Inc., and members of the local community. Ponds were excavated, wetlands cultivated, bridges erected, paths laid, filtration systems constructed, and trees, shrubs, and wildflowers planted. Thanks to more than a decade of such activity, Terraview-Willowfield stands today as an award-winning and precedent-setting model for ecological restoration and stormwater management efforts.

The northernmost end of Terraview Park stands less than two hundred metres from Highway 401. It is here, just off Pharmacy Avenue, where raw stormwater pours into Terraview from the surrounding area. These waters are channelled into a renaturalized oasis, a wetland populated by such natives as tamarack, staghorn sumac, flowering raspberry, elderberry, mulberry, and chokecherry. This wetland

Habitat island in Terraview Pond

channel soon opens up into a large pond in which it meets with additional runoff flowing in from the surrounding residential community.

While Terraview Pond is certainly impressive to behold, its ecological function is nowhere near powerful enough to completely deal with the stupefying levels of polluted water that course through it. To further assist, Terraview sports a variety of technological features including French drains, oil/sediment separators, storm-water detention facilities, and an advanced subsurface filtration system located under Terraview's soccer field. Even the kids' splash pad, which overlooks the pond, offers its own filtration system so that the water it expels can be contributed to the pond.

At the southern end of Terraview Pond, the water flows into a renatural-ized creek bed and is transported under Penworth Road, emerging again in Willowfield Gardens Park where it meanders a hundred metres or so before reaching Willowfield Pond. The banks of Willowfield Pond are lined with a wonderful mosaic of plants, shrubs, and trees, planted by hundreds of volunteers over the years. Blackberry bushes grow in the shadows of trembling aspens. Cedar and elder rub elbows. Potentillas bloom next to young sugar maples. Hawthorn and dogwood frame patches of yarrow and Canada thistle. Thanks in no small part to

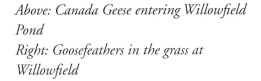

Above: Canada Geese entering Willowfield Pond
Right: Goosefeathers in the grass at Willowfield

this vital diversity of plant life, the pond also finds itself home to a variety of creatures including great blue herons, mallard ducks, Canada geese, and even the occasional muskrat.

At the southern end of this pond, visitors will find Terraview-Willowfield Public School. Students here enjoy some unique advantages given their proximity to Willowfield Pond. In fact, the layout of the pond was explicitly designed to provide outdoor classrooms and observations pods to enhance educational opportunities for students. The school's commitment to environmentalism and ecological literacy has earned it recognition by the Toronto District School Board as a Platinum level EcoSchool.

A small paved path in front of the school heads eastward to a pedestrian bridge.

Looking north across Willowfield Pond

This bridge crosses one of the more interesting and innovative aspects of the Terraview-Willowfield renaturalization effort: a peat bog stormwater management system. Waters from Willowfield Pond pass through this specially designed wetland in one final act of filtration before exiting the parkland. Looking down from the bridge, one can still see the remnants of the old concrete channel peeking out from amongst the cattails, before the waters are carried off south along the old hydro corridor.

There is absolutely no question that Terraview-Willowfield's restored and enhanced ecological function does much to improve the water quality of Taylor-Massey Creek. Sadly, however, the creek remains one of the most polluted waterways in Toronto, and in all of Canada. Along its journey to the Forks of the Don, Taylor-Massey Creek is assaulted by illegal sewer hookups, contaminants from the local community, heavy urbanization of the creek passage itself, and the severe degradation and elimination of historic stormwater ponds and wetlands. When it meets with the Don River, it delivers the sum of this tragedy there, and by extension to Lake Ontario. Improving the water quality of Taylor-Massey Creek may well be one of the most significant acts imaginable to benefit the Lower Don River. Terraview-Willowfield, if nothing else, should serve as a solid reminder of just how much is possible when we set our collective minds to addressing these issues.

CHARLES SAURIOL
CONSERVATION RESERVE

11

The East Don River passes under Lawrence Avenue just east of the Don Valley Parkway (DVP). As it does so, the river crosses the northern boundary of the Charles Sauriol Conservation Reserve, an impressive swath of urban forest and important bio-corridor that stretches all the way down to the Forks of the Don.

Toronto pays homage to Charles Sauriol in many ways. A parkette on Broadview Avenue bears his name, as once did a trail in the Rouge Valley (now officially called the Hillside Trail). In 1995, the Oak Ridges Moraine Land Trust and Metro Toronto and Region Conservation Authority founded the annual Charles Sauriol Environmental Dinner to help raise funds in support of conservation activity. Outside the city, conservation areas near the Credit River, Lake Opinicon, and in Norfolk County all honour his legacy. The reason for all this is simple: Sauriol was one of the most passionate conservationists, dedicated stewards, and earnest environmental advocates Ontario has ever known. His words and actions had an enormous impact on both the city and the province, helping not only to preserve

Commemorative marker at south end of reserve by the Forks

and restore countless hectares of wilderness, but to transform the very way people thought about our natural world.

Charles Joseph Sauriol fell in love with the Don Valley in his early teens, following camping trips in the area with his Boy Scout troop. In 1927, he secured a lease on a small property at the Forks of the Don, roughly where the southern end of the Charles Sauriol Conservation Reserve is today. Here, at his little cabin, he built a bee yard and wildflower garden, tapped sugar maples for syrup, and mounted his own reforestation efforts to restore the barren lands left behind by nineteenth-century settlement.

By 1946, Sauriol's love for the valley prompted him to co-found the Don Valley Conservation Association (DVCA), an environmental organization devoted to protecting and preserving the Don Valley. A few years later, he began publishing *The Cardinal*, a modest quarterly journal dedicated to the natural heritage and local history of the area, and the official voice of the DVCA. Sauriol had first tried his hand at assembling this material in book form, but publishers rejected it on the

East Don River in Milne Hollow

grounds that no one would be interested. *The Cardinal* was launched in 1951 and remained a going concern until March 1956.

When Hurricane Hazel tore through the Don Valley in October of 1954, its devastation landed right on Sauriol's doorstep. The cabin survived, but the Don Valley would never again be the same. The aftermath of the storm provoked the government to reconsider its approach to flood protection and water conservation and inspired the formation of the Metro Toronto and Region Conservation Authority (MTRCA) in 1957. The previous December, Charles Sauriol had been approached by Metro chairman Frederick Goldwin Gardiner (after whom the Gardiner Expressway is named) and asked to serve as the chairman of the Conservation Areas Advisory Board of the MTRCA. Sauriol, of course, accepted.

Working with the MTRCA over the next decade and a half, Sauriol played a pivotal role in orchestrating many notable acquisitions, including land at Albion Hills, Bruce's Mill, Claremont, Cold Creek, Duffins Creek, Roblin's Mill, and throughout much of the Don Valley. In 1958, his own cabin at the Forks was expropriated by the MTRCA to pave the way for the DVP, and Sauriol migrated to the other side of the river, occupying the former homestead of Captain Phillipe de Grassi, originally erected in 1831. Ten years later, another MTRCA expropriation moved him from this property as well.

Old Milne homestead

Sauriol left the MTRCA in 1971 for a full-time commitment with the Nature Conservancy of Canada (NCC). In 1982, he became their executive director and remained in this role until his retirement in 1987. Until his death on December 16, 1995, Sauriol continued to champion the conservation and reclamation of our wilderness. Of particular significance was his success in securing what is now the Todmorden Mills Wildflower Preserve, co-founded with his friend Dave Money, past president of the Ontario Horticultural Association.

At the northern end of the Charles Sauriol Conservation Reserve lies Milne Hollow, once the site of Milneford Mills, the residence and enterprise of Alexander Milne, who built on the land in 1832. A small Gothic Revival farmhouse from this time still stands today, barely recognizable as a historic building thanks to subsequent occupation right up until 1992.

Milne Hollow is beautiful. Thanks to outstanding restoration efforts by the resident stewardship group and Local Enhancement and Appreciation of Forests (LEAF), the site is populated by wonderful specimens of serviceberry, cup plant, white oak, hickory, and native phragmites. Invasive phragmites sprout here as well,

The Rainbow Bridge

as do other non-natives like purple loosestrife, common buckthorn, garlic mustard, and common tansy. Stewards battle the invasives year after year, and slowly native asters, goldenrod, wild bergamot, grey-headed coneflower and Michigan lily are taking their place. The meadowland at Milne Hollow is recognized as an important resource for migratory birds and is an official site of the Toronto Bird Flyways project.

South along the trail from Milne Hollow and across the East Don sits a tunnel pushing under an old railway line, leading the trail onwards to Moccasin Trail Park. This iconic portal is Toronto's beloved Rainbow Bridge, a site that everyone who's ever taken the northbound lanes of the DVP is no doubt aware of, a splash of childlike colour popping up from the scrub along the highway. The rainbow was first painted in the early seventies by Berg Johnson, a teenage immigrant from Norway. Johnson felt Torontonians too dour, too serious, and hoped a little colour and frivolity would brighten their day. The city frowned upon this and covered it up with a coat of monotone grey. Undaunted, Johnson restored the work dozens and dozens of times over the next two decades, suffering four arrests in the process.

Purple loosestrife

Finally, thanks to efforts of community organizers, the rainbow is now an officially sanctioned art work, maintained at least in part by the city itself.

The vast expanse between Milne Hollow and the Reserve's southern edge at the Forks of the Don has proved itself one of the most vital bio-corridors in all of Toronto for as long as anyone cares to remember. On those rare occasions when the local news reports a white-tailed deer found wandering the downtown streets, there's no small chance that at least part of its journey took it through the Charles Sauriol Conservation Reserve. For humans, however, journey through these lands has not been such a simple matter over the last several decades. Attempts to stitch together an official, contiguous path through the reserve have been scuttled and frustrated time and time again.

Official trails are established in Toronto by a set of basic principles. The impact to the natural environment, both during construction and routine maintenance, must be minimized. Flooding and erosion control measures must be accounted for. Steep grades are to be avoided whenever possible. Site accessibility must be considered. Costs must be strictly controlled. For the Charles Sauriol Conservation

Developed trail through Charles Sauriol Conservation Reserve

Reserve, these factors may be the least of its challenges. The reserve approaches or intersects with many private and commercial properties, including lands or infrastructure owned by the Canadian National Railway, Flemingdon Golf Course, Hydro One, and Enbridge Gas. Gaining the support and co-operation of all the various stakeholders (or at least their lawyers and insurance providers) has proved a complex, multi-faceted and, all too frequently, insurmountable problem.

In May 2012, a feasibility study was completed to assess whether winding part of the East Don Trail through the Charles Sauriol Conservation Reserve could finally connect its southern- and northernmost edges. Potential design concepts were developed and subjected to public consultation throughout 2013 and 2014. With luck, you will one day be able to walk this trail yourself.

BROOKBANKS PARK AND DEERLICK CREEK

Deerlick Creek flows through residential and semi-industrial land from its head-waters near Highway 401 just east of the Don Valley Parkway until it joins up with the East Don River in Chipping Park, just north of Lawrence Avenue.

From York Mills south to Cassandra Boulevard, Deerlick Creek flows through Brookbanks Park. The north end of Brookbanks is primarily a recreational area, sporting a well-paved trail that leads past a children's playground with all the usual equipment and a very popular splash pad. Heavy recreational use coupled with extreme proximity to the neighbourhood leaves obvious signs of the challenges this area faces. The nearby woods support a very sparse understory thanks to vicious erosion from neighbourhood stormwater overflow, rogue foot traffic from visitors, and the ravages of their off-leash pets. This exposed dirt also magnifies Brookbanks' ongoing trash problem. It is commonplace to find the nearby woods littered with an assortment of debris and refuse: potato chip bags, old soda bottles, chunks of Styrofoam, candy wrappers, old cigarette packages, you name it.

Above: Looking toward the playground area
Right: Discarded bike in Deerlick Creek

There are, of course, ongoing efforts to protect and nurture the area back to more vigorous health. Like most of Toronto's green spaces, Brookbanks benefits from periodic community clean-up events. City workers actively maintain the grounds and inspect the nearby woods for any significant changes in tree health or soil condition. The creek banks have enjoyed numerous infrastructure improvements and renaturalization projects over the years, as seen in the great diversity of native shrubs, grasses, and wildflowers that line the creek and crawl atop its armour stone walls.

South of the playground, Brookbanks begins to transform to a wilder space, something more analogous to how it might have looked before urbanization pounded at its borders. From the trail, visitors might spot red cedar, yellow birch, white pine, sugar maple, or blue beech popping up across the landscape. Where the understory has thickened, mayflower, buttercup, wild ginger, Solomon's seal, ostrich fern, and trout lily all rise from the earth, competing as they can against encroaching invasives like common buckthorn and dog-strangling vine. In wetter spots, you can easily steal a glance of turtlehead, marsh marigold, cattail, and joe pye weed.

Deerlick Creek

Canopy of maple leaves

For several seasons in the late 1980s and early 1990s, Dr. Mima Kapches of the Royal Ontario Museum conducted a variety of archaeological digs in some of the backyards that line the Brookbanks Park ravine. During a dig in the fall of 1987, she uncovered a Meadowood cache blade dating from 1,000 BCE, making it one of the oldest ever discovered. Continued excavation the following year uncovered a variety of Middle Archaic period artifacts, including a small pebble that displayed a human face in effigy, believed to have been created in 4,700 BCE, making it one of the oldest-dated human representations in northeastern North America. From 1988 to 1990, digs in an adjacent backyard revealed a wealth of Early Iroquoian pottery (ca. 1,000 CE), as well as the remnants of a site that would have been used in its production. These discoveries have led local archaeologists to hypothesize that the ravine surrounding Deerlick Creek may have once served as a seasonal pottery production and firing campsite.

Brookbanks Park is bisected by Brookbanks Drive, a roadway that winds its way through the surrounding neighbourhood from Ellesmere Road before becoming Three Valleys Drive on the western side of the Don Valley Parkway. Deerlick Creek curves westward to parallel the road for a few hundred metres before being channelized under the road and emerging on the other side.

The southern section of Brookbanks is strongly similar in natural composition to the section to the north, but sadly, it suffers from a far greater intensity of use.

A murmuration of starlings

A multitude of ad-hoc trails and short cuts carve across the forest floor from the apartment complex that looms over the western slopes. With these trails comes a notable increase in trash and refuse, which all too often includes broken furnishings and houseware, items that were obviously walked into the forest and discarded with an ignorance bordering on malice.

Despite the disregard some choose to show this sensitive wilderness, local wildlife struggles to carry on with its daily business. Hairy and downy woodpeckers are often heard hammering away in the canopy above. Murmurations of starlings flit from tree to tree. Raccoons, skunks, and groundhogs wander the forest floor, questing for food and shelter. In decades past, there were even sightings of red squirrels and short-tailed shrews, although neither have been reported in quite some time.

Given the impressive diversity of local flora and fauna, fascinating archaeological discoveries, and a tie-in to the local museum, you'd expect to find informative and educational signage throughout Brookbanks to bring all this to life. Sadly, as is too often the case in Toronto's ravines, the signs that do exist pay lip service at best to the area's local history and natural heritage.

Deerlick Creek being channelized under Brookbanks Drive

Toronto's wilderness and green spaces are part of the city's core identity, and have been since its very foundation. The beauty and abundance that drew native peoples to our rivers and hilltops also romanced early European settlers, encouraging them to settle in the area. Thousands of years of human history have unfolded in our woods, and yet you could walk these trails today and learn next to nothing about any of it. You might find a sign presenting the name of an eighteenth century hamlet, sketches of a few local plant species, perhaps even passing mention of an important event from a century or two ago, but details would be scant, and words too few.

Trail signage offers amazing opportunities to profile the history of our lands, to celebrate individuals who have richly contributed to the city, to ignite passions for ecological concerns, and to foster support for city and community initiatives that aim to understand or improve our natural areas. Yet for decades, places like Brookbanks are adorned with minimal, generic signage, vague and uninspired. If we hope to inspire protection and care for these areas in our communities, the rich history and heritage of our natural spaces should be found on the trails, not trapped in the pages of a book like this one.

THE LESLIE STREET SPIT AND TOMMY THOMPSON PARK

Tommy Thompson Park is a unique and dynamic part of Toronto's urban wilderness. The park occupies much of the Leslie Street Spit, a five-hundred-hectare constructed peninsula composed primarily of decommissioned construction materials and detritus dredged from Toronto's outer harbour. Popular opinion is that the spit was needed as a place to dump all the debris and fill collected from various construction projects around the city, but that's arguably a half-truth. With construction of the Saint Lawrence Seaway underway, city planners imagined a huge increase in shipping traffic on Lake Ontario and speculated that a breakwater would be essential for managing the conditions in the Toronto harbour. Thus, in the late 1950s, a tiny finger of land began a five-kilometre crawl out into the lake. As it turned out, the advent of intermodal shipping containers a few years later would render the need for the breakwater virtually obsolete. Conveniently,

*Above: Shoreline formed by
construction debris
Right: Plant life takes hold
amongst rust and refuse*

however, the two decades of fran-
tic urban growth that Toronto
would soon experience validated the need for the spit when it began to serve as a
resting place for uncountable tons of construction rubble and clean fill.

Life on earth is nothing if not gregarious. As soon as the spit began to take
shape, a multitude of plants and animals started to colonize this new land. Balsam
poplar and eastern cottonwood appeared in discrete thickets peppering the landscape. Viper's bugloss, scouring rush, and Canada thistle settled into what could
soon be called true meadows. Purslane, sandbar willow, and lamb's quarters grew
alongside the developing dunes and barrens. By the mid-1970s, nature's wonders
were as evident on this artificial headland as the materials used in its formation.

The spit became a hot-button issue in the 1970s. At the start of the decade,
access was tightly controlled by the Toronto Harbour Commissioners (THC) and
firmly off limits to the public. Community pressure built steadily year after year,

Western shore of Tommy Thompson Park, facing lighthouse

and by 1973, the THC began running Sunday bus tours that permitted Toron-tonians some level of site access. Increased public interest, not surprisingly, soon attracted city developers who imagined rapidly expanding the land mass to create a profit-rich aquatic destination, serviced by a small airport and filled with marinas, sailing clubs, and water play facilities. Local institutions like the Toronto Field Naturalists, as well as thousands of concerned citizens, quickly rallied to prevent commercial development on the spit and lobbied for increased public access. By 1977, most of the efforts to industrialize and commercialize the spit had been squashed, and a policy of public access on weekends was instituted. That same year marked the foundation of the Friends of the Spit, an organization that continues to advocate on behalf of the spit's natural beauty to this day.

Originally planned to be little more than a finger-like breakwater stretching into Lake Ontario, the spit stands today as a rugged and ever-growing tapestry of lagoons, peninsulas, coves, lobes, and embayments. The ad-hoc nature of the spit's construction, coupled with a decades-long program of innovative ecological enhancement, has given rise to a densely-packed mosaic of habitats defined by dramatic changes in landscape features and soil composition. Forests and thickets, populated by balsam poplar, trembling aspen, and red osier dogwood, provide shelter and stomping grounds for hoary bats, Virginia opossum, and raccoons. Vast

Above: Eastern cottontail
Right: Muskrat

meadows host groundhogs, meadow voles, and eastern cottontails, who scamper amongst the boneset, tansy, chicory, and goldenrod. Sand barrens and dunes can be found dotted with the footprints of deer mice and graced with patches of common mallow, Canada bluegrass, and pearly everlasting. Cattail, coontail, purple loosestrife, and Richardson's pondweed sprout up across wetlands frequented by muskrat, beaver, mink, Blanding's turtles, and leopard frogs. Combined, this remarkable crossroad of human agency, native flora and fauna, and invasive species forms a complex, novel ecosystem unlike almost anything else to be found in the Greater Toronto Area.

The spit's unique nature and location have given rise to Tommy Thompson

Important Bird Area (IBA) seen from afar

Park as an ideal venue for a staggering diversity of biological research and monitoring projects. Scores of vegetation surveys, water and sediment samplings, wildlife breeding studies, butterfly and bird counts, and numerous other assessments and investigations have all been conducted in the park by agencies and academics from across North America.

Of all the research and study being conducted along the spit, none is more notable than the work related to its prolific and thriving bird communities. Since the turn of the millennium, more than three hundred distinct species of birds have been identified on the spit — a greater inventory than has been found in the more remote and protected environment of Algonquin Park. In 2000–01, the Leslie Street Spit was designated an Important Bird Area by BirdLife International, providing breeding grounds for over 6 per cent of the global population of ring-billed gulls and an estimated 30 per cent of the domestic population of black-crowned night-herons. In 2003, the Toronto and Region Conversation Authority (TRCA) established the Tommy Thompson Park Bird Research Station to help further the study and protection of avian life. From here, thousands of birds from dozens of species are logged and banded each year. If for these reasons only, the park enjoys a considerable international reputation, something that Toronto would be wise to promote and protect.

Gulls nesting on beach at edge of IBA

Tommy Thompson Park is, absolutely, a birder's paradise. Huge populations of golden-crowned kinglets, white-throated sparrows, and myrtle warblers all patronize the spit. Common terns nest on habitat rafts in the northernmost embayment and interior lagoon. Robust colonies of double-crested cormorants can be found on virtually every peninsula. Red-tailed and sharp-shinned hawks glide and drift above the spine road. Snowy owls perch upon the rocks of the endikement. Even more regionally rare visitors, like Virginia rails, American woodcocks, and yellow-throated vireos, are spotted with some frequency. The best birding in Toronto is here, and requires nothing more than binoculars and time.

While birds are the focus of the most extensive research conducted along the spit, the park's Urban Coyote Study should be considered of equal importance. Coyotes were first noted at the Leslie Street Spit in 1993, observed both at the baseland area near Unwin Avenue and out by the automated lighthouse at Vicki Keith Point to the south. The TRCA, in partnership with the Ministry of Natural Resources, has since devoted significant attention to the study of the canid population in Tommy Thompson Park. This research has led to many interesting insights about territorial fidelity, space use, habitat requirements, and use of connective corridors in and out of the park. Many of the coyotes who are being tracked for ongoing study have been equipped with collars, but as dogs are not allowed anywhere in Tommy Thompson Park, there is little chance that uninformed visitors will mistake them for off-leash pets. Coyote sightings should be reported to park naturalists whenever possible.

Embayment wetland

Even though Tommy Thompson Park is an ecological trust of great sensitivity and importance, it remains highly accessible to the public. Some areas, like the forested baselands near the main parking lot, offer many earthen trails from which to explore the park and take in the sights. Paved side trails provide hikers safe transport through a variety of other locations. The central spine road (car- and truck-free during public visitation hours) offers cyclists a convenient and enjoyable route across the whole spit, from its intersection with the Martin Goodman Trail to the toplands in the far south. Pedestrians are well-advised to stay alert for bike traffic whenever they find themselves near the spine road. While all recreational trails in Toronto have bylaw-mandated speed limits of twenty kilometres per hour, more than a few cyclists on the spit opt to ignore it. Speedbumps have been built in several locations but vigilance remains the watchword when visiting the spit on foot.

THE FORKS OF THE DON

The Forks is perhaps the single most important geographic feature in the Don Valley, a physical nexus that unites Toronto's wilds like no other. The West Don River, fed by such notable tributaries as Wilket Creek and Burke Brook, winds its way through the city from headwaters near Maple, Ontario, to terminate its journey here. Similarly, the East Don River snakes its way down from headwaters near Yonge Street in Richmond Hill, picking up the waters of Deerlick Creek, German Mills, and other tributaries before coming to an end here as well. Hardly two hundred metres to the east of where these branches meet, the waters of Taylor-Massey Creek complete their journey from headwaters near Terraview-Willowfield, passing into the flow of the East Don River. At the Forks, these watercourses merge to become one, the Lower Don River.

At the northern edge of the 36,000-hectare Don watershed is the Oak Ridges Moraine, one of the most vital and ecologically important landforms in southern Ontario. Waters from here begin a thirty-eight kilometre journey through the GTA to Lake Ontario, growing in volume as millions and millions of litres of rainwater, municipal runoff, and sewage overflow drain into the Don River

Taylor-Massey Creek meets the East Don River

system. A seemingly endless cast of tributaries fuel this flow along the way: Patterson Creek, Cummer Creek, Duncan Creek, Westminster Creek, amongst others. Each of these watercourses deposits its own trickle, harvested from the streets, fields, backyards, parking lots, homes, and businesses that populate the surrounding communities. This way, drop by drop, the bulk of the water to be found in the Don watershed passes through the Forks. And with it, evidence of the millions of us who call this city home passes through the Forks as well.

The Forks is not only a meeting place of water, but of parklands. Across the arched pony truss that spans the East Don River, you'll find the southernmost point of Charles Sauriol Conservation Reserve. To the north it is bordered by E. T. Seton Park. Stroll past the mouth of Taylor-Massey Creek and under the Don Valley Parkway and you'll immediately find Taylor Creek Park and Coxwell Ravine Park. Pick up the Lower Don Recreational Trail as it overlooks the meeting of the East and West Don and you're mere minutes from Crothers Woods and the Beechwood Wetlands.

The siren call of the Forks extends back in time, as well. Lieutenant-Governor

Above: East Don River with pony truss
bridge in background
Right: Trailside at the Forks

John Graves Simcoe and his wife, Elizabeth, no doubt wandered the woods that would have surrounded the Forks in the late eighteenth century. Decades later, the Helliwell family would have ventured upstream from their nearby settlement at Todmorden Mills. Captain Phillipe de Grassi, who lent his name posthumously to a certain fictional school, took possession of eighty hectares at the Forks (then called the Boatbildery) in 1831. Part of his land was eventually sold to the Taylor family, generations of whom tromped through the area, passing from residence to business, as required. In the early twentieth century, the Forks served as a routine camping spot for local scout troops, as it did for the likes of E. T. Seton and Charles Sauriol. By 1947, Sauriol was a permanent resident of the Forks, owner of a small lot purchased from the Canadian National Railway.

Walk the Forks today, however, and virtually nothing exists to inform or educate passersby as to the staggering importance this area holds. In warmer months, there is hardly a moment of daylight where two strangers would not pass one

Noel Harding's Elevated Wetlands

another on its network of trails, paths, and roads, and yet, for most, the Forks is largely a mystery, a stepping-stone between destinations, not a destination of its own. In fact, when describing the location of the Forks, natural landmarks prove far less effective than one simple question: "Do you know those giant molars along the side of the DVP?"

Erected by the Canadian Plastics Industry Association in 1998, Noel Harding's *Elevated Wetlands* is a series of sculptures that borders the Don Valley Parkway. Part art installation, part renaturalization effort, and part marketing initiative, these intriguing forms were used to lionize the plastics industry by filtering the local river water, at least in theory. How effective they were in achieving this noble goal may be hotly contested, but there is virtually no doubt that they now represent the most iconic feature of the Forks, and are a landmark recognized city-wide. Without them, the Forks might well be cursed with a complete and undeserved anonymity, relegated merely to a dip off the side of the highway or an intersection of recreational routes leading elsewhere.

E. T. SETON PARK

E. T. Seton Park is located west of Don Mills Road, stretching roughly from Eglinton Avenue south past Overlea Boulevard and into the Thorncliffe Park area. It is named after Ernest Thompson Seton, an influential force in the foundation of the Boy Scouts of America, and author of several works inspired by a youth spent in the Don River valley. Seton was responsible for donating part of the current parkland to the city following his death on October 23, 1946, one of several reasons the area bears his name today.

Coursing through the length of the park, you'll find the West Don River, en route down to the Forks only a kilometre or two farther south. Its sandy banks, and the heavily treed valley slopes to its west, offer habitat to red squirrels, rabbits, coyotes, foxes, groundhogs, and even to deer and beaver on occasion. White pine and white spruce share sunlight with staghorn sumac and various types of maple and oak. Throughout, exotics and invasives mass and spread, with garlic mustard, dog-strangling vine, purple loosestrife, crack willow, and phragmites easily spotted from virtually every view and vista along the way.

This wilder side of the park stands in stark contrast to the manicured lawns

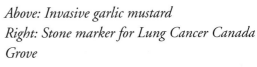

Above: Invasive garlic mustard
Right: Stone marker for Lung Cancer Canada Grove

and strategic treescaping that comprise much of the eastern side of the river. Here, weeping willows and sugar maples abound, many offering shade to the benches that lie sheltered beneath their limbs. Scores of these trees sport commemorative plaques honouring the memory of deceased loved ones, or attempting to further the reputation of the company that paid for their planting. This is particularly the case in Lung Cancer Canada Grove, a section of cultivated parkland found in the northern section of the park, some three hundred metres east of the elevated railway bridge that stretches high above the valley.

Thanks in part to this clash of landscapes, E. T. Seton Park enjoys a reputation as one of the top bird-watching locations in the city. Eagles, red-tailed hawks, and American crows can be spotted with very little effort or patience soaring in

Above: Songbird meadow with bird boxes
Right: Bird tracks along the banks of the West Don River

the skies above the park. American redstart, wood thrush, veery, and even the occasional pair of scarlet tanagers are all known to use the surrounding woods as breeding grounds. Great horned owls, pileated woodpeckers, blue jays and northern cardinals perch in the branches above, watching as northern flickers and red-breasted robins forage on the ground below them. Birding opportunities in the park have been intentionally fostered by way of strategic plantings. The most notable example of this can be found along the western edge of Lung Cancer Canada Grove, where a songbird meadow has been populated with black-eyed Susan, cup plant, and goldenrod, as well as a multitude of wooden nest boxes that rise up between the wildflowers. Here it is not uncommon to spot ruby-throated hummingbirds, white-throated sparrows, eastern meadowlarks, and American goldfinch amongst a multitude of other species.

What makes this swath of green space most noteworthy, however, is not its ecological importance, but its recreational importance. E. T. Seton Park offers a combination of opportunities that can be found nowhere else in the city. The park

Hole one of disc golf course

offers a one and a half kilometre, eighteen-hole disc golf course, which opened in 2011. Biking, rollerblading, skiing, and horseback riding were all considered when planning and paving its path and trail routes. Geocachers have come to use the fields and woods to host the trappings of their sport. Picnic areas are plentiful, and it is even still possible to find fire pits, a feature becoming increasingly scarce throughout the city.

The development of the park's recreational facilities stems from a legacy established in the very earliest days of the city's stewardship of the land, and one set in motion by E. T. Seton himself. When Seton willed the land to the city in 1946, one of the stipulations was that it would remain responsible for maintaining a public archery range on the site, or else see the land return to the Seton estate. As a result, to this day the Toronto Public Archery Range still stands in E. T. Seton Park, the only free, public range in this city, and one of the few in all of North America.

Decades later, much of this parkland became scheduled to serve as the home of the Toronto Zoo. By 1964, that plan was squashed, however, and architect Raymond Moriyama was commissioned to design the Centennial Centre of

Target butts at the Toronto Public Archery Range

Science and Technology to sit on the site instead. Construction was originally intended to conclude in 1967, to coincide with Canada's Centennial celebration, but various delays conspired to waylay its opening by approximately two years. In light of this, the name was changed to the Ontario Science Centre, which opened its doors on September 26, 1969.

Between the Toronto Public Archery Range and the Ontario Science Centre, there can be little doubt that E. T. Seton Park will remain a strong candidate for recreational development in the city, particularly for activities that benefit from a more natural setting than many urban parks may offer. Attempting to balance heavy recreational use with cultivating and protecting natural habitats should be seen as an ongoing opportunity for innovation in land use and stewardship. Here, we may well discover new ways to encourage reclamation and renaturalization of urban space across the city, specifically in those contested cases where NIMBYism, zoning conflicts, or the desire for economic development might otherwise prevent progress.

EDWARDS GARDENS AND WILKET CREEK PARK

16

When Alexander Milne arrived in 1817 in the area surrounding what is now Lawrence Avenue and Leslie Street, he walked amongst towering stands of white pine, sugar maple, and red oak to gaze upon the babbling waters of Wilket Creek. White-tailed deer and black bears wandered these woods, nourished by the bounty of the raspberry, blackberry, and mulberry that soaked up sun in verdant, fertile thickets. To early pioneer families like Milne's, such sights must have seemed a gift, a welcome reward for the risks and trials of settlement. Given a grant of five hundred acres by the Crown, Milne, a Scottish weaver, quickly determined that the creek was ideally suited to serve as host for his new home and enterprise.

By 1827, the creek had come to be known as Milne Creek, and upon it stood a three-storey woollen mill, the first of its kind in the fledgling city. The family home was erected on a nearby hill, and the lands cleared in its construction were seeded with crops to better secure sustenance for the cold Canadian winters. The creek, however, did not perform as Milne had hoped. Diminished in volume over

Gravestone of Alexander Milne, William Milne, and his wife Jane Weatherstone, hidden in Edwards Gardens

several seasons, Milne was forced to uproot the operation in 1832, moving all that mattered to a new location on the East Don River, in what is now the part of the Charles Sauriol Conservation Reserve dubbed Milne Hollow. The family, however, continued to occupy the land along Wilket Creek for a century to follow. Alexander Milne was laid to rest here, at the age of ninety-nine, and his gravestone still stands overlooking Edwards Gardens, located just off the southwest corner of the parking lot.

In 1944, these lands ended up in the possession of industrialist Rupert E. Edwards. Edwards spent considerable time and expense transforming the land into a sprawling garden and private nine-hole golf course. He had four hundred tons of limestone shipped in from the Credit River Valley, built bridges, dams, and ponds, and constructed artificial hills. It is said that Edwards did all this with the intention of seeing it become a public park, which came to fruition when the city purchased the land in 1955. However, speculation is strong that financial hardship and frustrated exhaustion may have been a larger motivation for Edwards to ditch the property. Whatever the reason, Torontonians gained much when the property fell into the public trust.

The manicured state of Edwards Gardens remains today much as it did in the

Native species bed in Botanical Garden

1950s. Ornate rock gardens and flower beds punctuate tracts of open grass. Roses and rhododendrons bloom with violent colour. Fountains gurgle in small ponds sporting a near-impossible diversity of plant life. Gazebos and trellises offer shaded refuge from the heat of summer. Metasequoia, a most unusual redwood, cast long, stark shadows across the fallen snow in winter.

Not everything, however, is as it was in Edwards's days. In 1998, the Garden Club of Toronto helped establish the Teaching Garden atop the slopes on the western side of the creek. This impressive facility provides children with educational programs designed to foster love and passion for all things green. The Sensory Garden teaches them to appreciate nature not only with their eyes, but their noses, mouths, and fingers. The Spiral Butterfly Garden, which frames a sculpture of a giant monarch butterfly, enlightens them on how the sun's movement affects the growth and spread of plant life. An herb garden brings plants into a culinary context. Perhaps most important of all, two large vegetable gardens serve to educate the youngsters on food from field to table, with the garden's abundance donated to a local food bank as it ripens.

Similarly, back in 1958, the Garden Club of Toronto founded the Toronto Civic Garden Centre on the site, which was replaced by the Toronto Botanical Garden in in 2003. Dominating the northeastern corner of Edwards Gardens,

Dawn redwood at Edwards Garden

Above: Giant monarch in the Toronto Teaching Garden at Edwards Gardens Left: Toronto Botanical Gardens at Edward Gardens

the Toronto Botanical Garden offers over a hectare of beautifully arranged planted plots and terraces, outdoor sculpture, topiary, carpet beds, artificial nests and hibernaculum, a cafe (built on the foundation of the original Milne house), as well as educational facilities. A multitude of themed gardens present visitors with a dense mosaic of unique landscapes, bringing together native plants like black-eyed Susan, joe pye weed, and purple coneflower to stand in contrast with more exotic specimens like European copper beech, Danford iris, and Griffith's spurge.

Dog-strangling vine

Botanical gardens, in one form or another, have existed for millennia. Royalty in ancient times would often reserve grounds on which to display plants of reputed medicinal or economic value, the spoils of their exploration or conquest of remote kingdoms and lands. By the seventeenth century, such gardens began to demonstrate a growing devotion to the science of botany, and plants were no longer selected only for their perceived value, but also for their more academic or aesthetic merits. While these endeavours have greatly expanded our knowledge of botany and satisfied the immense curiosity of researchers and layfolk alike, they have not been a purely beneficial invention. More than a few of these captive exotics have not remained so for long. It is said that a wealth of troublesome invaders were introduced to our lands by North America's botanical gardens. Dog-strangling vine, for example, is rumoured to have been one such escapee, although origin stories do differ from source to source. Contemporary botanical gardens, however, like the Toronto Botanical Garden, now maintain strict selection and cultivation practices in hopes of preventing such accidents.

Between the Toronto Botanical Garden and the grounds of Edwards Gardens, visitors may be given the impression that wildness is not a treasured characteristic of the area. Opinion is transformed, however, by a quick stroll to the southern edge of the property, where the creek flows into Wilket Creek Park. These ravine

Wilket Creek in Edwards Gardens

lands have largely escaped the pressures of human endeavour and urbanization, having enjoyed a protected status as city parkland since 1928. By the end of the 1940s, much of the area north of Lawrence was farmland, and Leslie Street would starkly cleave through what was then called the Barber Greene Woods, paving the way for much of the community we see today. Yet this small corridor along Wilket Creek seems to have survived more or less intact. What remains is certainly not pristine, but it has fared much better than many. Here, you are surrounded by mature forest, populated by varieties of maple, oak, beech, hornbeam, willow, and hemlock. Scattered throughout the understory are some very rare plant species such as snakerod and sicklepod, as well as more common species like daylily, cattail, wild succory, milkweed, all-heal, and cow vetch. Follow the trail to its end and you'll arrive in Sunnybrook Park, one of Toronto's most popular recreational green spaces.

LOWER DON RECREATIONAL TRAIL

17

In her famous diary, Elizabeth Simcoe (the wife of Lieutenant Governor John Graves Simcoe) describes the Don Valley of the 1790s as an idyllic place, an unspoiled wilderness fed by the flow of the great Don River and its tributaries. Here, salmon-rich waters flowed past glades of white pine and butternut trees that towered over cockspur hawthorn, partridgeberry, and sweet-scented ferns. Bald eagles stalked the waters in search of food, perching upon the branches of the poplars and basswood that rooted themselves on sugarloaf hills overlooking the river. Deer wandered rolling meadows where swarms of tiger swallowtail butterflies flitted from flower to flower. Even in winter, the frozen waters of the Don provided an ample bounty as residents pulled countless red trout from holes carved through the ice.

By the late nineteenth century, the unrelenting growth of the city had rendered much of the Don Valley a grotesque contradiction of the native beauty it had once been celebrated for. Raw sewage poured into the river, mixing with industrial

Above: City shed along Lower Don Recreational Trail south of Pottery Road
Left: "Don Was Here" art installation by John Loerchener and Laura Mendes, part of the Eco-Art-Fest, 2014

effluent and waste from the various tanneries, abattoirs, refineries, and agricultural concerns that occupied the valley. The towering pines that had once so impressed early European settlers had largely been cut down, replaced by a wave of white oak and scrub brush. The unbearable stench of the river wafted over what remained of this once bountiful landscape, now wounded by the primitive industrialism of the time.

Back then, many folks still believed that disease was born from "bad air" released by rotting organic matter, so the Don, and to a larger extent the Ashbridge's Bay Marsh into which the river flowed, were seen as the source of many epidemics that washed across the city. Cholera, diphtheria, and a form of malaria that residents knew as "lake fever" all routinely threatened the local population and, consequently, the river was viewed as an affront to the safety of the community.

The contempt many early Torontonians felt for the Don was prompted by more than just pollution and disease. Over the nineteenth century, the valley had

Railway crossing over the Lower Don

also earned a reputation as a home for the city's criminal element and indigent population. Shacks, shanties, and ditch dwellings dotted the landscape, serving as home to the city's less fortunate. The notorious Brooks Bush Gang, responsible for numerous vile acts including the murder of a member of provincial parliament in December 1859, were known to haunt the woods, preying on those who dared to travel on nearby streets. Gang member James Brown would become the last criminal to be publicly hung in the city, on March 10, 1862. Two years later, construction of the Don Jail was completed, an architectural monument that would serve to connect the Don River with crime and violence in the minds of the citizenry for decades to follow.

When a major storm rolled through town in September 1878, the flooding — the worst the city had endured in over a quarter century — proved a proverbial last straw in the city's relationship with the river. Public discussion as to what could be done to remedy the problems associated with the Don began to escalate and intensify. Commercial interests, eager to see the Don opened up to increased rail and ship traffic, were quick to jump on board the building momentum, adding their voices to the chorus. By early 1881, municipal government and local business owners had become enamoured with a rather drastic scheme: to straighten, widen, and deepen the Don River.

Straightened section of the Lower Don seen from northern end

The so-called improvement of the Don was imagined to have all manner of benefits: it would increase the speed of its flow, reducing stagnation and improving sanitary conditions, and it would support greater volumes of water, leading to better flood control. The plan called for various allotments along the new watercourse to open up economic opportunities, which would be driven by the potential for larger ships and better connections with the railways. Commercial developments would bring new life to the area, driving away the undesirable communities that had taken root in the valley. On paper, the plan seemed full of promise.

By October 1886, municipal council had acquired all of the permissions to proceed with this radical transformation of the Don. By spring of 1887, the project was in full swing, the valley abuzz with dredging machines, pile-drivers, barges, horses, and innumerable workers armed with picks and shovels. From Winchester Street south to Lake Ontario, a large, straight channel was dug, the excavated materials used to fill in the curves and bends of the natural river course, forcing the waters to adopt the new trench as its new path down to the lake.

As you might well imagine, given the complexities involved, all did not go exactly as planned. An unforeseen abundance of shale and clay plagued the digging with difficulty and made it impossible to see through to specification. Work

Dame's rocket

was started, stopped, reassigned, and rescheduled due to labour complications. Political disagreements prompted delays in negotiations and problems with pay schedules. When the project was finally completed in 1892, years after its delivery date, the costs had more than doubled compared to original estimates. More importantly, the benefits of the project were nowhere close to what sponsors and city residents had hoped for. Some problems lessened and new opportunities did present themselves, but in the final analysis, the Don Improvement Project delivered little more than an ugly scar carved through what had once been a place of great beauty.

Today, people who wish to examine this relic of urban planning can do so with ease from the Lower Don Recreational Trail, a multi-use, paved trail that shadows the Lower Don River along a narrow strip of land on the western bank, wedged between the river and the railroad tracks. The portion of the trail that follows the straightened segment of the Don offers little to enjoy other than a wonderfully convenient path through the city. The thin ribbon of vegetation, with the exception of a few planted meadows and thickets, is overrun by the worst of our invasives: dog-strangling vine, garlic mustard, dame's rocket, wild succory, and Japanese knotweed. The roar of the Don Valley Parkway serves as an ever-present

Lower Don Recreational Trail crossing at Pottery Road

aural backdrop, punctuated by the footfalls of recreational runners and the ringing bells of commuting cyclists. The trail, certainly, is not without its charms, but it is far more a transit corridor than a leisure destination.

North of the straightened segment, however, the Lower Don Recreational Trail is freed from such narrow confines and begins to provide more abundant natural beauty. Immediately north, you enter the area Elizabeth Simcoe wrote so frequently about, the part of the valley that would have surrounded Castle Frank, the Simcoe's summer residence. Farther along, just south of the Prince Edward Viaduct, you pass the venerable Chester Springs Marsh, one of the flagship renaturalization efforts found along the Don. On the other side of the viaduct, the trail soon crosses Pottery Road and weaves its way along the borders of Crothers Woods and the Beechwood Wetland to arrive at the Forks of the Don. From Castle Frank Brook to the Forks, visitors will find well-wooded tracts still populated by beech, maple, and basswood, a token reminder of what was sacrificed to accommodate the straightening of the Don.

CROTHERS WOODS AND BEECHWOOD WETLAND

18

Two blocks east of where Broadview curves to become O'Connor Drive, a small side street begins its steep descent into the Don Valley. After crossing beneath the Don Valley Parkway, where you will discover the Toronto Police Service's canine academy, Beechwood Drive loops back around on the west side of the DVP. At one point in the not-too-distant past, this road was one of several long-standing routes that allowed transit into and across the Don Valley. Today, the bit of Beechwood Drive that runs south of the canine academy is inaccessible to cars, but continues to allow hikers and cyclists a route into this area of the Don Valley, home to both Crothers Woods and the Beechwood Wetland.

About three hundred metres south of the underpass, the road makes a sharp right and quickly intersects with the Lower Don Recreational Trail. To the immediate southeast of this intersection, protected by a three-beam wooden fence that curves to follow the length of the trail, you'll discover the Beechwood Wetland. The Beechwood Wetland is amongst the more noteworthy restoration efforts ever

Lower Don Recreational Trail leading past Beechwood Wetland

completed in Toronto. Thanks to over a century of agriculture, decades of industrial activity, the construction of the DVP, and essentially unchallenged conquest by invasives like garlic mustard, Japanese knotweed, and dog-strangling vine, this area was, at one point in time, a disaster. Restoration planning began at the turn of the millennium, bringing together participants from various organizations, including the Federation of Ontario Naturalists, the Task Force to Bring Back the Don, the Toronto and Region Conservation Authority (TRCA), the City of Toronto Parks and Recreation, the Ministry of Natural Resources, and the McCutcheon Family Charitable Trust. Heavy machinery was deployed in 2002 to help improve the flow of water from groundwater seepage and street runoff, as well as to radically transform the surrounding topography. In the years that have followed, countless volunteers have donated their time and labour to maintain and improve the Beechwood Wetland. These efforts have yielded great reward. It is now a thriving home to leopard frogs and snapping turtles, visited by coyote and foxes, and populated by vibrant patches of wild raspberry, goldenrod, and staghorn sumac. Little nooks along the trail give convenient views of the wetland and offer impromptu seating

Above: Railway crossing near Cottonwood Flats
Right: Staghorn sumac

and better-than-average information signs.

Passing west through the intersection of Beechwood Drive and the Lower Don Recreational Trail, the old road leads visitors across a very active railway line and into Crothers Woods. In the early nineteenth century, part of the nearby area was known as Terry's Field, named after Parshall Terry, who built a home here around the time of his election to the first parliament of Upper Canada. This home was eventually moved and rebuilt closer to Pottery Road and is now preserved as part of the Todmorden Mills Heritage Museum.

Other famous Ontarians set up residence in the nearby area throughout the nineteenth century, including Major David Secord (Laura Secord's brother-in-law), who built a sawmill on the banks of the Don River in 1815. Most influential in the development of Crothers Woods, however, was the Taylor family, who built a homestead here in 1826, near Beechwood Drive and the DVP, and who would go on to purchase Terry's Field around the dawn of the twentieth century.

Bridge over Lower Don to Sun Valley

Terry's Field then found itself a part of the brickwork enterprise of the Taylor Family, in part thanks to a partnership with Sir Henry Pellatt, the builder of Casa Loma. The Sun Brick Company Limited conducted business here until some time in the late 1930s when the Town of Leaside took over the near-exhausted quarry. The land was soon condemned to serve as the town dump, a role it played throughout the 1950s and 1960s. By the mid-1960s Sun Valley was receiving hundreds of truckloads of garbage a day. When the trucks stopped arriving in May 1965, the site was estimated to have accumulated some eight hectares of industrial waste and sanitary landfill, compacted up to twenty-five metres deep in some spots. The site was then forced to accept ash from the Commissioners Street incinerator, a last spit in the eye to the pristine wilds that had once dominated the entire valley.

This story is similar all across Crothers Woods. Just half a kilometre northeast of Sun Valley stands the North Toronto Wastewater Treatment Plant, which has processed tens of thousands of cubic metres of effluent daily since it opened on August 1, 1929. Until 1979, the northwest edge of the ravine slope at the end of Redway Road was home to the Crothers Caterpillar plant, whose manufacturing of heavy machinery left industrial relics scattered throughout the nearby woods, some of which continued to be unearthed even decades later. At the foot of Beechwood Drive once stood Bate Chemical and Polyresins, who left behind soil so contaminated that it needed to be scraped up and shipped out en masse before

North Toronto Wastewater Treatment Plant

the area was deemed safe for use by Toronto Police Services. The Pottery Road snow disposal site, located directly west of the railway tracks in the area known as Cottonwood Flats, has accepted countless snow dumps over the years, each bringing with it a special toxic blend of road salt, antifreeze, motor oil, and other road-forged detritus. If you locate any place in Crothers Woods where more than a couple consecutive hectares of land have escaped human impact over the last two hundred years, consider yourself very lucky.

Despite all of this, nature has a way of enduring. Scattered across the fifty-two hectares that constitute Crothers Woods you can still find a surprising number of century-old sugar maples, white oaks, and American beech. Small enclaves that appear unchanged over hundreds of years pepper the landscape, where black walnut, blue beech, ironwood, and basswood loom over a robust understory of bloodroot, jack-in-the-pulpit, trout lily, and trillium. Crothers Woods is also known to support a number of regionally rare species such as greater straw sedge, poke milkweed, thin-leaved sunflower, and pale-leaved sunflower. Thanks to this diversity, and the rarity of species found within it, Crothers Woods was designated an Environmentally Significant Area (ESA) by the TRCA in 1995.

Being granted ESA status offers some protection against use or development that might be incompatible with the preservation of local habitat and natural features. But this protection assumes the area will continue to be used for recreation.

Signage along bike trail

For Crothers Woods, recreational use can hardly be considered inconsequential. Throughout the 1960s and 1970s, the area was quite popular with motorcyclists. These were largely displaced when mountain biking gained popularity in the 1980s. By the end of the millennium, some ten kilometres of riding trails had been carved out of the flats and slopes, many with little to no consideration given to ecological concerns or long-term sustainability. Designating Crothers Woods an ESA was an important first step towards preserving its natural heritage and ensuring its continued use, but it was far from the most important.

In July 2007, following a decade of studies and reports and years of public consultations with organizations like the Toronto Field Naturalists and the International Mountain Bicycling Association, the Crothers Woods Trail Management Strategy was finally unveiled. This master plan initiated a new course for the future of Crothers Woods, a future much brighter than might have been imagined only a decade or two before. Recreational use of Crothers Woods would be strongly influenced by ecological matters, ensuring both increased protection and restoration of the natural environment, while at the same time increasing recreational opportunities within the area. The plan was particularly pleasing to cyclists, as it served to enshrine Crothers Woods as a flagship destination for off-road biking, a recreational use given little reserved land elsewhere in Toronto's network of green spaces.

This space is for the birds

Above: Songbird meadow in Cottonwood Flats
Right: Birdhouse in Cottonwood Flats

Since the trail management strategy was unveiled, ecological enhancement and restoration efforts in the park have gained a steady momentum. One very noteworthy project can be found on the northern edge of Cottonwood Flats, just off the path that leads to the river crossing en route to Sun Valley. Here you'll find a small songbird meadow, easy to identify by the iconic signage that decorates the surrounding fence. The meadow was designed to attract the area's diverse avian community, known to include eastern wood-pewee, gray catbird, and chestnut-sided warbler. An assemblage of sitting stones makes it an attractive rest stop for human visitors as well.

A final note to visitors to Crothers Woods: while many of the trails are officially declared as multi-use, hikers are strongly encouraged to limit themselves to the larger paths that run through Sun Valley and Cottonwood Flats. Several well-used trails span the woods from Pottery Road to the Leaside bridge, but these are amongst the few challenging courses that exist for off-road cyclists in the city. Safety concerns aside, wandering here on foot can limit the enjoyment of those who came to ride the trails. In the spirit of friendship, community, and responsible use, let these trail users have their fun.

TODMORDEN MILLS WILDFLOWER PRESERVE

19

The oxbow trail through the Todmorden Mills Wildflower Preserve might very well be one of the most wonderful fifteen minute hikes Toronto has to offer. The trail encircles what was once a U-shaped bend (called an "oxbow") in the natural course of the Don River, which was severed off in 1959 when the river was rerouted to facilitate construction of the Don Valley Parkway. It's an area of significant historic interest, great natural beauty, and one of the most immediately accessible examples of the challenges faced in renaturalizing our urban environment. And, at about half a kilometre in length, it's the type of amble that can be squeezed into even a busy day.

The nine-hectare Wildflower Preserve is located within the greater acreage of the Todmorden Mills Heritage Museum grounds, which was established in May 1967 thanks to the passionate lobbying of the "grandmother of East York" Mayor True Davidson and venerable Toronto naturalist Charles Sauriol. The museum lands (coupled with nearby Crothers Woods) have served as home to some very

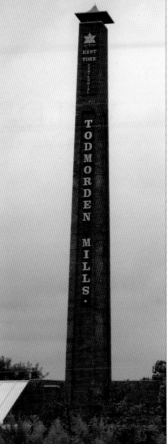

*Above: Cup plants in the meadow straddling the oxbow
trail
Right: Chimney at Todmorden Mills Museum*

important characters and industries of early Toronto history. It was in this area that, at the end of the eighteenth century, Isaiah and Aaron Skinner constructed the first grist mill on the Don River, using mill stones and irons bequeathed to them by then lieutenant-governor John Graves Simcoe. By 1823, the Helliwell family brewery and distillery would be built nearby, and the area would come to be called "Todmorden" after the Helliwells' home back in Lancashire, England. Only a few years later, one of the very first machine-made paper mills in Upper Canada would open its doors, producing (amongst other things) newsprint for such important publications as William Lyon Mackenzie's newspaper, *The Colonial Advocate*. By 1855, the Taylor Brothers York Paper Mill (or "Lower Mill" as it was more often called) would stand on the site. From this area once flowed Toronto's most coveted staples: flour, paper, and booze.

Oxbow trail through the forest edge

During the first few decades of the twentieth century, Todmorden served as an extension of the nearby Brick Works. Damaged and defective bricks were carried by horse from the Brick Works and deposited throughout Todmorden. It's said that the old brewery was filled two floors deep with old bricks at one point, and that the original road bed into the site was built on a few metres of discarded brick. To this day, visitors can still easily spot old bricks jutting up from the earth in random spots about the site.

During World War II, Todmorden found itself playing host to a prisoner-of-war camp. Members of the German merchant marines were housed in tents and huts while labouring at the nearby Brick Works or Greenwood clay pits. Although, according to True Davidson's biography, calling it a POW camp might be a bit harsh: "I remember being told by a long-time resident of East York that these were very low-risk prisoners, mostly merchant seamen caught in Commonwealth ports when war was declared. The internees worked in the brickyards and . . . often socialized with their guards and residents of the community after work in the bar at the Todmorden Hotel at the top of Pottery Road hill." The prisoners were released and repatriated at the end of the war, and the camp itself was trashed by vandals shortly thereafter. The last remaining camp structures fell to arsonists in March 1946.

Discarded brick from nearby Brick Works

Over the next forty-odd years, Todmorden would be forced to endure a relentless assault inflicted upon it by the growing city. Materials excavated during the construction of Toronto's subway system were dumped throughout the nearby areas of the Don River valley, radically transforming the natural systems at work. The homes and agricultural businesses that once dominated Broadview Avenue were replaced by apartment buildings, automotive repair shops, and restaurants. The ravine soon became home to countless discarded tires, cinder blocks, bits of broken furniture, and reams of other refuse, by-products of industry and ignorance, left to rust and rot just slightly out of sight. The construction of the Don Valley Parkway would set Todmorden awash in road salt, cigarette butts, and drifting trash from the nearby highway.

The environmental degradation of the site gave birth to a novel and decidedly non-native ecosystem. Where once you would have found fine specimens of white pine, balsam poplar, and red oak dominating the landscape, by the 1980s, the area was virtually overrun by invasive species such as Manitoba maple, black alder, Japanese knotweed, buckthorn, wood avens, dame's rocket, garlic mustard, and Himalayan balsam. This radical transformation of habitat, coupled with ever-increasing vehicular traffic surrounding Todmorden, depopulated the area of much of the wildlife that had once called it home. Beavers, raccoons, groundhogs, and muskrats became depressingly few and far between. They were replaced by a swelling

Himalayan Balsam

collective of feral cats and aggressive legions of invasive European fire ants.

In 1990, Charles Sauriol and Dave Money, past-president of the Ontario Horticultural Association, began discussing how the fate of Todmorden might be rewritten. By 1991, the pair had helped form the Todmorden Mills Wildflower Preserve Committee (TMWPC), a charitable organization that would serve to empower a passionate volunteer corps to protect and renaturalize the site to whatever degree possible. In doing so, they helped to establish a legacy of environmental stewardship that would remain for years a model of what a determined and persistent group of grassroots conservationists can achieve when given the opportunity.

It is estimated that at the turn of the millennium, some 75 per cent of the biomass at Todmorden consisted of invasive or introduced plant species. This was, by many estimates, a notable improvement over where things had stood less than a decade beforehand. Year after year, Todmorden volunteers continued to support a cycle of cleanups, plantings, weedings, and eradications aimed at fostering succession by native species. According to the *Todmorden Mills Environmental Baseline Study* conducted by James Kamstra in 2003, of the 375 species of vascular plants identified on the site, approximately 240 species were regionally native, with some 150 of those having been introduced to the site as a part of these restoration efforts.

The volunteers remain hard at work even today. Entering the oxbow trail from

Todmorden stewards removing huge stand of invasive Japanese knotweed

the southern end of the parking lot leads you along the edge of a lush and lovely meadow, populated by an abundance of species including Canada anemone, wild bergamot, Michigan lily, Canada columbine, grey-headed coneflower, Canada goldenrod, cup plant, Kentucky bluegrass, heath aster, and sharp-lobed hepatica, to name only a handful. Certainly, these natives still wrestle against an onslaught of invasives, including ox-eye daisies, cow vetch, and the dreaded dog-strangling vine, but compared to what stood here when Sauriol and Money founded the TMWPC, the difference is remarkable.

The trail then arcs eastward into the nearby forest and soon ascends a short flight of stairs. Sugar maple, American elm, trembling aspen, eastern cottonwood, and silver maple, as well as regionally rare red cedar and slippery elm, can all be found scattered from the marshy edges of the oxbow all the way out to the southern end of the site by Chester Hill Road. Scores of species occupy the understory including such interesting fellows as riverbank grape, Virginia waterleaf, jack-in-the-pulpit, white trillium, chokecherry, hedge bindweed, bloodroot, and heart-leaved aster. These woods are also known to support one of the largest populations of skunk cabbage in the Greater Toronto Area, providing an outstanding vision in early spring as the plant's ability to generate its own heat lets it surface from the snow far in advance of its neighbours.

The upland forest soon gives way to wetter, more swamp-like habitat.

Above: Oxbow trail through the upland forest
Left: Ostrich fern

Natural springs, coupled with runoff from the streets above, create intermittent watercourses that flow down from the steep valley walls and into the oxbow. Swamp milkweed, Jerusalem artichoke, marsh marigold, red osier dogwood, cow parsnip, spotted jewelweed, fringed loosestrife, joe pye weed, and a variety of ferns including marginal wood fern, Christmas fern, and ostrich fern, can all be found throughout the area. Moss-covered logs lie strewn about in abundance, serving as home to countless creepy-crawlies as well as majestic examples of bracket fungi and other mushrooms.

Next up along the trail is the spectacular Todmorden Pond, which came into

Above: Todmorden Pond
Right: Red-eared slider turtle

being in 1994 after volunteers enhanced and deepened a large natural depression, hoping it could serve as vital habitat for a variety of local flora and fauna. Efforts were quite successful it would seem — sitting by the water's edge your vision is filled by cattail, duckweed, and patches of blue flag iris in bloom. Depending on time of year, the air may be filled by a chorus of green frogs glugging away their banjo-like calls and splashing about in search of food. American toads and snapping turtles are both now residents of Todmorden Pond as well, as is at least one red-eared slider turtle, likely someone's abandoned house pet.

From the pond, it's hardly a two-minute stroll to the northwestern edge of the preserve, which is actually the official trailhead. From 1967 until 2008, the historic Canadian Pacific Don Rail Station was located here. The station is now in Roundhouse Park, near the foot of the CN Tower. Many of the other buildings that comprise the Todmorden Mills Heritage Museum are located here, however, and offer an easy visit after a very lovely stroll.

GLENDON FOREST

20

At over sixty hectares, Glendon Forest ranks amongst the largest forests in the city of Toronto. Designated an Environmentally Significant Area (ESA) by the Toronto and Region Conservation Authority (TRCA) in 1982, it is a vital habitat for a variety of regionally rare plant and animal species, and serves as one of the most important bio-corridors in the West Don River valley. Its mix of woodland and wetland is home to over forty different vegetation communities, at least thirty-seven species of rare flora, and over a hundred species of fauna. Its substantial wetland provides significant water storage and is an important breeding ground and migratory stopover for many animal species. Glendon Forest's vital ecological functions are felt far outside the bounds of the forest proper.

In a practical sense, it might be more apt to discuss Glendon Forest as two separate places: the area located predominantly to the west of the river and the region on the opposite side of the Don, often referred to as "the east." The western side supports a paved path and formal signage, and connects with nearby locations such as Sunnybrook Hospital and the Glendon College Campus of York University. The opposite side of the river is a wilder domain, far more isolated and far more fragile.

Above: Entrance to Glendon Forest in Sunnybrook Park
Right: Bull thistle

The southern trailhead of the paved path is located in Sunnybrook Park. At the beginning of the twentieth century, this area was the northern end of Sunnybrook Farm, the estate of Joseph Kilgour, president of the Canada Paper Company Limited. Kilgour's widow, Alice Margaret Kilgour, donated the Sunnybrook Farm property to the city in 1928 for use as a public park, and their barn still stands only a hundred or so metres to the east of the trailhead.

The lands that border the path introduce a telling narrative if you know how to read it. Native red oaks loom over patches of invasive bull thistle. Magnificent sugar maples stand next to thick, troublesome patches of Japanese knotweed. Orange jewelweeds blossom a stone's throw from their unwanted cousins, glandular touch-me-not. Bitter chokecherries peek out amongst the hypnotic leaf pattern

Above: Japanese knotweed
Left: Invasives dominate native plants
along an impromptu trail

of dog-strangling vine. Here, like in countless places in the Toronto area, a vicious war is being fought between native and invasive species. In wilder ecosystems, such skirmishes would be limited to fringes and forest margins. In the more novel ecosystems in our urban centres, however, the forest is essentially all margin, even in a place as seemingly well-preserved as Glendon. The war rages everywhere.

Roughly half a kilometre from the Sunnybrook access point, the path takes visitors past Glendon's largest wetland site. Within, you can find boneset, St. John's wort, joe-pye weed, and turtlehead alongside more commonplace residents like duckweed, elderberry, and red osier dogwood. Of course, invasives are no less present here than elsewhere in Glendon: blooms of yellow iris and sprawling stands of phragmites rise and fall across the landscape. Visit in late spring and you're sure to be treated to one of the wetland's most remarkable treasures: teeming, swarming

Above: Green frog
Right: Tadpoles in Glendon
wetland

masses of green frog tadpoles numbering in the thousands. As you might suspect, many other creatures look forward to this annual explosion as well: red-winged blackbirds, belted kingfishers, and snapping turtles, all of which frequent the wetland.

Soon after the wetlands, visitors will encounter the first bridge that crosses the West Don River as it flows through Glendon Forest. Continue along the paved path and you'll find yourself enjoying a pleasant amble along the Don, eventually skirting the Glendon College athletics field and arriving near Proctor Field House and the college's parking lot, which empties on to Lawrence Avenue East. Cross one of the bridges, however, and you'll immediately find yourself in a wilder Glendon. Here, old growth abounds, and you can find outstanding examples of sugar maple, American

Old bridge crossing the West Don River

beech, American elm, eastern hemlock, and eastern white pine with virtually no effort. Its rich and diverse understory supports countless interesting plant species, including such natives as partridgeberry, starflower, leatherwood, fairy spuds, and silvery glade fern.

Don't be surprised, however, if you find the bridges fenced off, defended by chains, iron gates, and other barriers designed to forcibly restrict visitors. Sadly, Glendon is a proverbial poster-child for many of the threats facing our fragile urban forest, such as erosion, soil compaction, and destruction of habitat. The periodic erection of these ramparts is merely one of several desperate measures local conservationists are forced to take to protect our natural heritage.

Preserving our natural environment and keeping it accessible to the public is a challenging balance to strike. Recent history has shown that without passionate advocates, places like Glendon Forest are too easily treated like resources rather than as heritage, to the detriment of the environment. While some people are motivated to stewardship by purely abstract inspirations, most require a personal, intimate

Broken gates on bridge to eastern side of Glendon

connection with these places before they are willing to dedicate time, money, or energy in their defence. To protect places like Glendon, we must encourage people to visit them and accommodate them when they do so, despite the fact that each visit comes at a cost to the very environment we seek to protect.

Such a strategy will work only if we all agree to be bound by the watchwords "responsible use." In Glendon, responsible use means this: stay on the established trails; obey posted signs; and keep your dog(s) on a leash. Conservationists have posted dozens of signs asking visitors to follow these rules, yet infractions still occur. Everything from wooden fences to massive iron gates have been erected to dissuade people from entering particularly sensitive areas, only for these obstacles to end up bent, broken, and bypassed.

Take the case of off-leash dogs, for example. When dogs wander off trail and their joyful romps can compact the soil, increase erosion, and damage native plant and animal populations; damage rare or endangered plant species; disturb wildlife nesting sites; and spread the seeds of invasive species. Off-leash dogs can frighten or hurt people, too, and cause confrontations. No one likes to think that their furry best friend could be harming the very place they have come to escape from the hustle and bustle of city life, but off-leash dogs are a top concern for conservationists.

Above: Paw prints off the path
Left: Typical dog on leash sign

The world behind the gates at Glendon Forest is worth protecting. Across the bridges there exists a remarkable, important, and fragile beauty. Pileated woodpeckers hunt on fractured trees riddled with moss and fungi. Olive-sided flycatchers sally and dart for prey in the wind. Tiny, intermittent watercourses carry water from springs and rainfall across the forest floor and down to the West Don River. Tiger swallowtails flit amongst the birch trees as eastern commas hunt for nettles along the river bank. Darkened nooks and folds frame the translucent white stalks of the incomprehensibly rare ghost plant. Hundreds of critters live, hunt, and breed in these woods, sustaining a food web that stretches from creature to creature in ways we can't even imagine. As is the case with all of our natural spaces, the greatest threat is our own irresponsibility, and the greatest mercy, our care.

MOORE PARK RAVINE AND THE BRICK WORKS

21

Moore Park Ravine stretches from Moore Avenue (across the street from the Mount Pleasant Cemetery Visitation Centre) down to the Don Valley Brick Works on Bayview Avenue, following the course of Mud Creek. With its historic headwaters located just east of Downsview Park, Mud Creek is one of Toronto's famous "lost rivers," a watercourse long buried under the asphalt and concrete of the developing metropolis. This ravine is one of the few places where Mud Creek still flows under the open sky, and even here, it only does so intermittently.

In the late nineteenth century, the ravine was home to a section of the Belt Line Railway, a commuter rail service composed of two distinct loops that connected downtown with the city's growing suburbs, areas that today we call Rosedale, Forest Hill, and Swansea, among others. The loop that passed through Moore Park Ravine (or Spring Valley, as it was then called) was often pictured in promotional materials advertising the railway. Its showpiece station, Moore Park, was located on the western side of the ravine just south of Moore Avenue. The Belt Line was

Mud Creek outfall in Moore Park Ravine

a short-lived dream, however. Economic recession, coupled with the advent of streetcars, all conspired to shutter the service in November 1894, after little more than two years in operation.

Across the trail from where Moore Park station once stood is a small patch of marsh known as Belt Line Pond. The pond formed over a century ago, likely a consequence of the construction of the Belt Line Railway. While non-natives like Norway maple and crack willow do dot the landscape, the pond area has managed to maintain a surprisingly healthy population of native species over the decades, including wonderful examples of white oak, red oak, and sugar maple. Restoration projects have enhanced this inventory with a diverse assortment of other native trees and plants, including white birch, northern pin oak, marsh marigold, white vervain, and sphagnum moss. Poison ivy also lurks nearby, as it does throughout the rest of Moore Park Ravine, as posted signs will attest to.

Farther south along the path, the Heath Street pedestrian bridge looms overhead. A popular belief holds that the original bridge was financed by John Thomas Moore, one of the gentlemen responsible for the Belt Line Railway and a land speculator so instrumental in developing the area that the neighbourhood to the west of the ravine now bears his name. This is likely not the case. Moore was responsible for financing the construction of two bridges in the area: the first spanning Moore Avenue (where the trail begins) and the second spanning the

Wood ducks negotiating the lily pads in Don Valley Brick Works Park

Vale of Avoca in Rosedale Ravine. Both have long since been demolished. Back in Moore's day, a timber trestle carried Heath Street pedestrians over the ravine, the construction of which Moore probably had nothing to do with.

The Heath Street bridge is only the first of three bridges that span the Moore Park Ravine. Farther south is a fairly typical railway bridge, virtually unremarkable save perhaps for its location. During the last ice age, what we now call Lake Ontario was a significantly larger body of water called Glacial Lake Iroquois, which formed from the impact of the Laurentide Ice Sheet on the rivers of the Saint Lawrence valley. The tracks above, which still carry east–west traffic across the city, were built to follow what was once the Lake Iroquois shoreline. Much of the surrounding land, and particularly that found south of the railway bridge, would have been under water 13,000 years ago.

The third bridge is Governor's Bridge, originally erected in 1923 to connect Rosedale to an undeveloped parcel of land subdivided around 1912. The early homes built in the Governor's Bridge area followed popular architectural trends in California at the time and earned the neighbourhood the colloquial nickname "Little Hollywood." But its deepest roots are in the political culture of the time. The subdivision was part-owned by Wallace Nesbitt, puisne justice of the Supreme

Weston Quarry Pond

Court of Canada, and its name is said to have been inspired by the neighbour-hood's close proximity to Chorley Park, vice-regal residence of the lieutenant-governor of Ontario.

Past Governor's Bridge begins the approach to the Brick Works. The Moore Park Ravine trail continues along the edge of the site, eventually curving to run parallel with Bayview Avenue before connecting with Park Drive Reservation trail in Rosedale Ravine. Long before this, however, a few paths and staircases branch off from the trail to provide convenient access to the Brick Works.

Around 1882, the story goes, a young William Taylor was digging post holes for a fence and discovered a wealth of clay, perfectly suited to brick making. Seven years later, the Taylor family (after whom Taylor-Massey Creek is named) started the Don Valley Brick Works. The bricks made here were apparently of outstanding quality, winning awards at the 1893 Chicago World's Fair and the Toronto Industrial Fair of 1894. In 1901, the Taylors sold the business to their relative-by-marriage Robert Davies, who reformed the concern as the Don Valley Pressed Brick Works Company.

On the night of April 9, 1904, the most famous fire in Toronto's history began near the corner of Wellington Street West and Bay Street. The Great Fire would claim only one victim, but consumed one hundred and four buildings in the time it took firefighters to gain control of the blaze. In the aftermath, construction

Above: Reclaimed factory area of the historic Brick Works
Right: Last remaining chimney of the four that originally stood at the Brick Works

bylaws changed radically, and the Don Valley Pressed Brick Works Company was called up to supply tons of building materials to the growing city. Massey Hall, Old City Hall, Osgoode Hall, Casa Loma, and the Ontario Legislature all include bricks from the Brick Works. At the height of its operations, over forty million bricks were produced each year and used in construction projects all across Canada.

What makes the quarry most interesting, however, is not the materials it provided, but rather what was discovered there during its excavation. As the quarry was expanded during the first few decades of operation, workers accidentally exposed geological evidence of great importance. The north slope of the quarry revealed two different layers of ice age sediment sandwiching other layers of material, which proved that a warmer climate had existed during the time in between. This may not sound like much, but typically, the enormous pressures of glacial ice sheets scrape away all evidence of these warmer periods.

Wild Bergamot

As a result, climatologists of the time had argued that there had been but a single ice age. The north slope of the quarry was physical evidence that ice ages were periodic, and geologist A. P. Coleman would use this evidence to ensure himself a page or two in the annals of history.

The majority of access points along the Moore Park Ravine trail lead to the Don Valley Brick Works Park, a city-operated green space built upon the site of the original Brick Works quarry. The park contains three small ponds, fed by a diversion pipe running in from Mud Creek, that form an important cornerstone in ongoing efforts to re-establish and improve the Don Valley watershed.

Countless volunteers have contributed to renaturalization efforts in the park over the years, working to shepherd ecological succession in this once heavily disturbed area by planting native flora and removing invasive species. Park wetlands now support dense arrangements of narrow-leaved cattail, as well as arrowhead and water lily. The woodlands along the slopes are home to sassafras, black cherry, sugar maple, and eastern redbud as well as Carolina rose, wild raspberry, chokecherry, and red trillium. Enchanting wildflower meadows host aster, black-eyed Susan, hepatica, wild bergamot, and evening primrose.

Through the Weston Family Quarry Garden at the southern edge of the park is the Evergreen Brick Works, a community environmental centre that occupies the reclaimed factory area of the historic Brick Works. In 2002, Evergreen, a national charity, conceived an idea to "launch a native plant nursery that would provide youth with employment and skills-development opportunities, propagate native

Hilltop path on eastern side of the Brick Works

plants that would support the delivery of our mission, and generate a financial return that would support our charitable mandate . . . a 'triple-bottom-line' enterprise that would provide environmental, social, and economic returns." Evergreen project manager David Stonehouse (who had also served on the Task Force to Bring Back the Don) suggested that the abandoned industrial complex at the Brick Works might serve as the perfect facility.

Over the years that followed, Evergreen, empowered by a passionate group of donors, volunteers, partners, and sponsors, have completely transformed the once derelict site into a harmonious and outstanding example of green design, social enterprise, and living heritage. Where once there was only rubble and refuse there now stands landscaped courtyards, a native plant demonstration centre, a thriving marketplace, community food gardens, and public event space. Year round, Evergreen Brick Works offers opportunities for individuals and families to participate in community events, workshops, and activities that focus on environmental appreciation, stewardship, and healthy living. With all this, the Brick Works represents an interesting alternate approach, combining conservation and responsible recreation, that is a worthy inclusion in the arsenal of options for protecting and preserving more of our urban greenspace.

EAST DON PARKLAND

22

For more than a few of Toronto's green spaces, there lies a gulf between what casual observers might define as its borders and what municipal authorities officially declare. Administrative paperwork and land surveys render boundaries with greater precision than may be evident at ground level. New parks are carved out from the old and bequeathed new names in celebration of historic or culturally important individuals. Trails are christened with names that connect them to their host park in ways oblivious to many visitors. Old signs stay in place, left in legacy as a cost-saving measure. Colloquial names sprout up that defy political oversight. Whatever the reason, it can be difficult to know exactly where you are, where one park begins and another ends, or where that trail at the side of the road is leading you today.

The East Don Parkland is an excellent example of this. A rogue sign for the park can be spotted along the western side of Don Mills Road, lonesome on the edge of another park that maps now call Betty Sutherland Trail Park. Ask a trail walker in the Bayview Woods–Steeles neighbourhood to name the green space you're in and you're as likely to hear of Garnier Park, Bestview Park, and Bayview Woods

Wetland near Newtonbrook Creek

as you are any mention of East Don Parkland. Enter the parklands from access points off some of the streets that border or intersect it, and you may encounter no signage whatsoever, leaving you only to discover the park's identity should you exit somewhere else.

Regardless, the descent into the shallow ravine at the northwest corner of Leslie Street and Sheppard Avenue is, by consensus if nothing else, the southern edge of the East Don Parkland. In the early 1800s, this area fell within the boundary of Clark's Settlement. The heart of the village, said to have been located half a kilometre to the southwest, supported a smithy, school, and church, but no tavern or hotel as village founder Thomas Clark was staunchly anti-liquor. Clark's home still stands today at 9 Barberry Place, protected under the *Ontario Heritage Act*. By the mid-1800s, Clark's Settlement had been absorbed by the expanding village of Oriole, a name still honoured throughout the surrounding neighbourhood.

Continuing northwards along the trail, visitors are eventually brought to the edge of Alamosa Park, by the courts of the Bridlebrook Tennis Club. In the days of Clark's Settlement, this area was close to Flynntown, a tiny village named after resident shoemaker Martin Flynn. As is too often the case, virtually all evidence of this small settlement has long since been dismantled or buried, but it is said to have been home to a few mills, a brickyard, various farms, and all the usual

145

Apple bloom

trappings of the early communities that sprung up along the Don River.

The trail then curves and weaves its way under Finch Avenue, through the hydro corridor, and on past Cummer Avenue before finally leading visitors to the ambiguous cluster of parks found in the Bayview Woods–Steeles neighbourhood. From there, the East Don Parkland proper bends to the east, eventually arriving at Leslie Street just south of Equestrian Court.

Taken in its entirety, the East Don Parkland is a spectacular and precious place, filled with beauty both subtle and grand. Black cherry and wild apple trees stand vigilant over sweet little meadows that teem with wildflowers and butterflies. Patches of wild strawberry grace the trail edges, their tiny white flowers highlighted in spring by the crimson leaves of last year's growth. Bracket fungi decorate the moss-riddled remains of trees lost to storms and age. All the while, the East Don River approaches the trail and retreats, peppered with babbling rapids that flow between undulating banks, scattered with rocks and stones of all shapes and sizes.

These expansive wilds are also home to several prominent wetlands. On the east side of the path near the mouth of Newtonbrook Creek stands one such example, a refuge to cattail, blue flag iris, and Canada anemone. South of Cummer Avenue

Above: Invasive phrag
Right: Phrag bed at the end of fall

is another, the product of a restoration and reengineering effort in 2008. Track the flight of passing ducks and herons to discover others, sequestered too far off the trail to be otherwise detected.

The moist meadows and thickets of the East Don Parkland, however, harbour a vicious, troublesome guest in the form of *phragmites australis* subsp. *australis*. By most accounts, the common reed (or "phrag" as many folks disparagingly call it) may well be Canada's most prolific and worrisome invasive species. Early records indicate that this towering perennial grass arrived in North America from Europe well over a century ago. By the 1940s, it had spread throughout the Saint Lawrence River valley and encroached upon the Great Lakes. Today, it can be spotted sprouting from wetlands, prairie sloughs, irrigation channels, and roadside ditches pretty much from coast to coast.

While invasives like dog-strangling vine and garlic mustard are certainly cause for major concern, in many ways phrag puts them to shame. Able to achieve heights of up to four or even five metres, dense stands (also called "beds") of phrag produce substantial shade, stifling neighbouring plants in their shadows. The plant's complex network of underground roots and rhizomes crawl forth from here, some measuring dozens of metres in length, spreading out to produce new shoots only a score of centimetres apart. Worse yet, phrag is allelopathic, meaning it releases toxins into the soil that essentially poison the land, further impeding the growth of nearby flora. The combined effect is nothing short of devastating.

From the outside, you might be inclined to view a large phrag bed as a verdant stand, possessed by a certain beauty as the reeds shift and sway in the passing breeze. Venturing into its interior, however, gives a startling appreciation for the devastation it brings. Inside, little else will grow, and biodiversity falls victim to the oppressive weight of the phrag monoculture. Small creatures like frogs and newts who mistakenly attempt to hunt and forage here may soon find themselves in peril, starving to death, lost in a green desert. Local hydrology is transformed, as the phrag's high metabolic and transpiration rates conspire to lower surrounding water levels and alter water cycles. Even in death, phrags lash out at the landscape by trapping nutrients extracted from the earth in their rigid, fibrous stalks, slowing the process of release to a crawl. Invasive phragmites are a scourge, and one that claims virtually incalculable hectares of treasured wilderness each year in its march of relentless assimilation.

Stewardship and conservation groups nationwide work diligently to push back phragmites' spread, but their actions are diminished by the plant's outstanding resilience and the lack of effective control options. Cut phrags down, uproot them, smother them in darkness, and you are just as likely to anger them as eliminate them. They are insidious, virulent, and largely irrepressible. Even the most hardcore naturalists are prone to confess that the responsible and judicious use of pesticides may be the only effective solution given the enormity of the problem. Pesticide use, however, is problematic and strictly controlled in many of the regions where it is so desperately needed. Meanwhile, fragile places like the East Don Parkland fall victim to phrags' spread, its territory increasingly occupied by aggressive and unwanted colonists riding in on wind, water, root, and rhizome.

ROSEDALE RAVINE

The Rosedale Ravine stretches from Mount Pleasant Cemetery southeast down to the Don Valley just north of the intersection of Bayview Avenue and Rosedale Valley Road. Entering these wilds via the northernmost access points found in either the cemetery proper or off nearby Heath Street, you are immediately delivered to a section of the ravine known as the Vale of Avoca, and the exact spot where the long-buried Yellow Creek emerges from its subterranean tunnel, part of the Belt Line Sewer.

Yellow Creek (sometimes called Sylvan Creek) is a historic tributary of the Don River, and has its headwaters up in Downsview. Like many of its brethren, it was buried as a part of storm-sewer construction long ago, and the Vale of Avoca is currently the only place where the creek still runs exposed to the open air. During rainstorms, the increased water virtually explodes forth from this outflow, tearing at the creek banks as it goes. As a result, much of the current creek bed has been lined with armour stone or gabion baskets to minimize the damage and stabilize the banks.

The Vale of Avoca suffers from severe erosion caused not only by the flow of

Yellow Creek erupting from Belt Line sewer

Yellow Creek and stormwater runoff from the streets above, but also from the large volume of pedestrian traffic the ravine endures. Joggers, hikers, commuters, commercial dog-walkers, school kids and campers, and myriad other visitors pound through the ravine almost every minute of the day, and well into the evening. To help protect this natural area from such extreme pressure, efforts have been made to marshal the flow of Yellow Creek as well as the flow of human visitation. The wooden boardwalks and stairs that run through sections of the ravine are there to eliminate foot traffic on the ravine floor, and visitors should stick to them strictly if they wish to continue to enjoy this remarkable part of the city.

Following the trail along, you quite quickly encounter the St. Clair Viaduct, a massive triple-arch bridge that carries St. Clair Avenue over the ravine, connecting the communities of Deer Park and Moore Park. An amusing bit of Toronto folklore worth repeating here is how St. Clair Avenue came upon its name. Back in the mid- to late nineteenth century, St. Clair was simply called the 3rd Concession Road. It passed through farmlands used by the Grainger family in and around Avenue Road. After watching a stage production of *Uncle Tom's Cabin*, a young Albert Grainger decided to adopt St. Clare as his middle name, in tribute to the character Augustine St. Clare. Alas, the theatre program incorrectly listed the character as Augustine St.

Elevated boardwalk protecting the ravine floor from human traffic

Clair, so this was the spelling that Albert used. To amuse himself one day, Albert erected a makeshift street sign on the 3rd Concession near Yonge Street that read "St. Clair Avenue." The name was quickly adopted by the community and eventually made its way into contemporary maps of the County of York.

The viaduct was erected in 1924 to replace an older iron bridge, built in 1890 by John Thomas Moore to open access to his fledgling subdivision, the neighbourhood we now call Moore Park. The original bridge started in the east almost exactly where the viaduct does, but crossed the Vale of Avoca at roughly a 45 degree angle, ending near the current intersection of Pleasant Boulevard and Avoca Avenue. After the bridge was demolished, some of its ironwork was integrated into the permanent fencing that presently separates the ravine's western slope from Avoca Avenue. An abutment of this bridge still exists today, and can be seen from the viaduct or by peeking down the eastern ravine slope from the small parkette on the corner of Inglewood Drive and St. Clair Avenue.

The area surrounding the St. Clair Viaduct exhibits an amazing mix of both native and foreign trees. Crack willow and Horse chestnut stand against a backdrop of black cherry and basswood. Stands of white pine and red oak are flanked by black locust and Norway maple. For the most part, particularly surrounding the creek itself, the understory is quite lush, populated by a variety of ferns, shrubs, and creeping plants. That said, the impact of sheet erosion on the western slope

Above: Ironwork from the nineteenth century bridge, reused as permanent fencing along Avoca Avenue
Left: Eastern abutment of original bridge

becomes increasingly severe the farther south you walk, and has essentially scoured some areas clear of understory altogether. Restoration has been attempted throughout the area, but to varying degrees of success.

The trail forks roughly half a kilometre from the viaduct, with the primary branch crossing Yellow Creek by way of a small footbridge, while the other provides access to Rosehill Reservoir, which sits atop the ravine slope. Constructed in 1873–74, Rosehill was Toronto's first major water reservoir, able to store close to 125 million litres of drinking water for the city. It was originally built open to the air, almost like an artificial lake, and was easily accessible from the surrounding community. In the midst of World War II, it was fortified through various means, including barbed wire fences, out of fear the site might become a strategic target. In 1966, following the Cuban Missile Crisis, the reservoir was expanded to handle over 200 million litres of water and was roofed to protect the water from

The gardens atop Rosehill Reservoir, as seen through Jack Culiner's iconic Galaxy

radioactive fallout in the event the Cold War turned hot. The following year, to celebrate Canada's centennial, a small park featuring a series of ponds and artistic fountains was completed on top the new roof, giving the site much of the appearance it enjoys today.

The primary branch of the trail on the east side of Yellow Creek soon crosses under an elevated railway bridge that spans the ravine along what was, some 13,000 years ago, the shoreline of Glacial Lake Iroquois. Roughly two hundred metres farther down the trail, Yellow Creek enters an inlet to become subterranean once again, this time for good.

Just past the inlet is the grassy recreational area of David A. Balfour Park. Technically speaking, the city has bequeathed the moniker David A. Balfour Park to much of the Vale of Avoca. Practically, however, when most people refer to David A. Balfour Park, they usually mean this small parkette, which stretches from the Yellow Creek inlet over to Mount Pleasant Road. Looking around the parkette, visitors might be compelled to conclude they have now reached the end of the Rosedale Ravine. This is not, in fact, the case. On the other side of Mount Pleasant Road lies the continuation of Rosedale Ravine, known as the Park Drive Reservation.

Park Drive Reservation was once part of a network of rudimentary roads that connected the Rosedale neighbourhood to the Don Valley proper. The completion of the Bayview Extension in 1959 and the construction of the Don Valley

Above: Rosehill Garden (in the park above Rosehill Reservoir) Left: Pale purple coneflower in butterfly meadow off of Park Drive Reservation

Parkway between 1961 and 1966 prompted members of the North Rosedale Ratepayers' Association to petition for the road's closure. In April 1973, the road was shut to public traffic, slated only for city workers to use to execute their duties.

Upon entering this section of Rosedale Ravine, you may note a small, overgrown meadow on the north side of the path. This renaturalized area was planted at the turn of the millennium specifically to serve as a butterfly habitat. Here, you may spot milkweed, cardinal flower, wild bergamot, and coneflowers sprouting up amongst fox sedges, buttonbush, and chokecherry, set before a backdrop of fragrant sumac and pussy willow. The host and nectar plants draw numerous species of butterfly, including eastern tiger swallowtails, monarchs, viceroy, and mourning cloaks. This habitat pays, in some small way, homage to amateur naturalist Paul Hahn, who was partially responsible for establishing the entomological collection at the Royal Ontario Museum. Hahn lived very nearby and is rumoured to have

The Spadina Storm Trunk Sewer and what remains of Castle Frank Brook

collected numerous specimens from in and around this area. East of the meadow, on the southern side of the trail, another large sewer outflow soon appears, barricaded behind a series of fences and rails. The waters that emerge from here are not those of Yellow Creek, as you might assume, but rather those of the Spadina Storm Trunk Sewer. This is what remains of Castle Frank Brook and a variety of its tributaries, increased in volume by the urban runoff from countless roads and sidewalks throughout Toronto. The path follows this channellized storm sewer for the remainder of its topside life.

Castle Frank Brook disappears back underground a few hundred metres past the Glen Road bridge, the sole roadway that crosses this section of Rosedale Ravine. Surrounding the inlet is a small nexus of paths heading off in various directions. Continue straight through this intersection and the trail will shadow the Bayview Extension as it makes its way to Evergreen Brick Works and up through Moore Park Ravine. Turn right instead, and you will find what remains of Milkman's Lane, a defunct road built in the latter half of the nineteenth century, which is said to have served as a popular route for dairy workers transporting product from the farms of the Don Valley. The road officially closed in 1958 and now exists primarily to transport ravine visitors topside to Craigleigh Gardens Park, once the residential grounds of late-nineteenth century member of federal parliament Sir Edmund Osler.

24

NORDHEIMER RAVINE AND GLEN EDYTH/ ROYCROFT WETLANDS

Like Cedarvale, Nordheimer Ravine is a natural space vastly remade in the wake of the Spadina Storm Trunk Sewer project and extension of Yonge–University–Spadina subway line. It is the effects of the latter that are the most visible at Nordheimer, and likely the reason many Torontonians are even aware of the ravine's existence. At 6:02 p.m. on August 11, 1995, two trains collided in the subway tunnels below, resulting in over one hundred injuries and three deaths. The Russell Hill emergency exit, located in the ravine on the western side of the Spadina Road bridge, played a pivotal role in rescue efforts, serving not only as an access and evacuation point, but also allowing emergency air conditioning to be deployed to combat the soaring temperatures in the tunnel.

To conservationists, the western side of the Spadina Road bridge is also known for another reason: the Nordheimer Skunk Cabbage Patch. Summoned into

Above: Russell Hill emergency exit
Right: Mouthwash bottle on ravine floor

existence by the dedicated efforts of the now defunct Task Force to Bring Back the Don, the patch is one of the largest of its kind in the city. Alongside the skunk cabbage, stewards helped to propagate other moisture-loving plants such as marsh marigold, spinulose ferns, and spice bush, establishing a significantly diverse understory that continues to struggle for ground today against myriad competitive forces.

While hunting for skunk cabbage and ferns, keen observers might notice something else in Nordheimer, particularly in the stretch between the Spadina Road bridge and the trailhead on St. Clair Avenue by the TTC station. All of Toronto's wild spaces struggle under the burden of litter and garbage, but the inventory at Nordheimer possesses a unique character. Mouthwash bottles are a mainstay, companions to a deluge of beer cans and bottles. Ziplock baggies, plastic bags, and glue tubes are comparatively plentiful. Sleeping bags and comforters are often easily spotted, wrapped in garbage bags, stashed under branches of white pine, or nestled into crooks provided by the man-made artifacts that occupy this natural world. While Nordheimer certainly has a reputation as a party ravine, the composition of

*Above: Homeless encampment at TTC emergency
exit off St. Clair West station
Left: Discarded beer bottle on ravine floor*

the ravine's trash equally points to use of a different sort — as a refuge for our city's homeless.

Toronto's ravines and urban forests have always played host to the city's indigent population. The Lower Don has a history of such spanning hundreds of years, and the same can be said for countless green spaces all across the city. These places offer privacy and isolation, and a safety of sorts from some of the commonplace threats the homeless are faced with on the streets of our concrete jungle. What makes homelessness in Nordheimer worthy of commentary is the stark contrast between the denizens of the ravine and the communities that encircle it. Nordheimer is surrounded by some of the most affluent neighbourhoods in all of Toronto: Forest Hill, Casa Loma, and South Hill.

On the eastern side of the Spadina Road bridge, Nordheimer meets with the grounds of Sir Winston Churchill Park and the St. Clair Reservoir. The reservoir was constructed in the 1930s to help improve the quality of Toronto's drinking water and to combat the city's growing water shortages. Unlike the open-air Rosehill Reservoir built atop Rosedale Ravine half a century beforehand, St. Clair

*Above: Sir Winston Churchill Park
and the St. Clair Reservoir
Right: View of trail under Spadina
Viaduct, seen from Sir Winston
Churchill Park*

Reservoir was fully enclosed from day one, the roof supported by a forest of concrete pillars. The architectural style and material engineering involved would serve to greatly inform the construction of the famous R. C. Harris Water Treatment Plant out in the Beach. Today, the slopes and surrounding area support a thriving plant community dubbed the Winston Churchill Savannah, a successful renaturalization effort that brought staghorn sumac, goldenrod, and a variety of native asters to the park.

The trail continues on east past the reservoir, the shade of the canopy falling away as it leads visitors to the Glen Edyth and Roycroft Wetlands. Glen Edyth is named after the mansion of Samuel Nordheimer (for whom the ravine itself is named), which overlooked the valley from 1872 to 1929. Both wetlands were established by the Toronto and Region Conservation Authority (TRCA) and the Task Force to Bring Back the Don in the late 1990s in order to help rebuild the Don

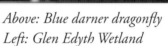

Above: Blue darner dragonfly
Left: Glen Edyth Wetland

River watershed. They serve as vital habitat for blue darner dragonflies, monarch butterflies, robins, and waxwings, and support a wealth of native plants and trees including Bebb's sedge, potato vine, Michigan lily, turtlehead, broad-leaved arrowhead, and red maple.

Erosion is a significant problem here, as it is throughout Nordheimer Ravine. The area is highly susceptible to all manner of erosive forces, not the least of which arrive in the form of human foot traffic and that of our canine companions. Off-trail wanderings have had a devastating effect over the years; scoured earth and tangles of exposed roots are easily visible. Given the popularity of the trail and the disregard some visitors show to posted signs promoting responsible use, there is, sadly, little doubt this damage will continue for the foreseeable future.

160

CEDARVALE RAVINE

25

For several months in late 1919 and early 1920, a young Ernest Hemingway lived on Bathurst Street, employed as a journalist for the *Toronto Star Weekly*. During his brief residence in the city, Hemingway took a fancy to the wilds of nearby Cedarvale Ravine, easily accessible to him via the muddy course of Bathurst Street, which crossed the ravine at ground level back in those days. Hemingway, still nursing shrapnel wounds received during his service in the Great War, would take constitutionals in the ravine, wandering past the buttonwood, elm, pine, and black locust that surrounded the flow of Castle Frank Brook.

Hemingway's Cedarvale was a very different place than what we see today. Gooseberry, black currant, and wild rice grew in abundance. Crayfish swam the waters of Castle Frank Brook. Cattle paths criss-crossed the ravine floor. Old growth was plentiful, with magnificent specimens of maple, hemlock, and oak to be found shadowing the landscape. What stands today, however beautiful it may be, is an area radically transformed by decades of urbanization.

By the 1940s, rural communities that had once seemed far removed from the hustle and bustle of downtown Toronto found themselves rubbing up against

Intermittent watercourse that once would have flowed into Castle Frank Brook

the edges of urban sprawl. Suburbia, in the form it took then, would soon be firmly entrenched in the growing city. City planners found themselves staring into the face of a vast and complex web of problems, most notably those related to transportation and sanitation. The usual humming and hawing morphed into a variety of proposals ranging from the pragmatic to the bizarre, but amidst the cacophony of debate, several solutions began to take shape that would change Cedarvale forever.

Shovels hit the soil in 1963 to initiate construction of a new highway that planners dubbed the Spadina Expressway. The expressway had first been proposed in 1949, and planning had evolved over the next fourteen years, shifting to revolve around a network of such roads, which included the Gardiner Expressway and Don Valley Parkway. In its final incarnation, the Spadina Expressway was an invasive and ambitious design, requiring the expropriation of hundreds of homes and the relocation of existing recreational parkland. So invasive was the plan that public outcry grew in tempo and volume the closer the construction efforts approached the neighbourhood of Humewood–Cedarvale. At the centre of the storm stood noted urbanist and activist Jane Jacobs, who had moved to Toronto in 1968 after successfully spearheading efforts to halt construction of New York's

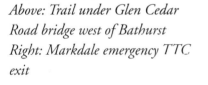

*Above: Trail under Glen Cedar
Road bridge west of Bathurst
Right: Markdale emergency TTC
exit*

Lower Manhattan Expressway. The inflamed passions of the local citizenry, coupled with Jacobs's battle-hardened resolve, proved a victorious force. By 1971, construction of the expressway was halted at Eglinton Avenue. The legacy of this project is what we now call the Allen Expressway.

While terminating the Spadina Expressway may have prevented Cedarvale Ravine from being paved over, parallel infrastructure efforts ensured it would never again be the same. As protests raged, workers were already on the ravine floor, in the process of burying Castle Frank Brook, stitching it into the fabric of the Spadina Storm Trunk Sewer. The extension of the Yonge–University–Spadina subway line in the 1970s brought "cut-and-cover" tunnel construction to the ravine — large tracts of wilds were clear-cut, dug up, and filled back in as the

Above: Cattail marsh by Bathurst bridge
Left: Cattail close-up

tunnel between Eglinton West and St. Clair West stations was built. These two monumental changes combined to permanently alter the hydrology and topography of Cedarvale, and in doing so changed the ecology of the entire ravine.

The large, open areas between the trailhead just outside St. Clair West station and the Bathurst Street bridge are, nowadays, predominantly wetlands, fed by numerous springs and intermittent watercourses that have been denied their traditional drainage opportunities. An impressive cattail marsh stands in the shadow of the bridge, bordered on all sides by a scattering of very old weeping willows. Further along the trail, it's easy to spot white spruce, cockspur hawthorn, Norway maple, Manitoba maple, and aspen rising up from the ravine's floor and

Above: Duckweed off side of trail
Right: Families in Nature

lower slopes. Yellow flag iris sprouts from duckweed-filled ponds that lie hidden behind the red osier dogwood, purple loosestrife, orange jewelweed, and greater lobelia that line the sides of the trail. Ecological succession is now a fait accompli, and the Cedarvale of old now largely annexed to the high slopes of the ravine.

As the trail emerges from the two-kilometre stretch of the ravine into Cedarvale Park, the landscape changes once again. The trees and plant communities that dominate the ravine give way to manicured grass, a soccer pitch, tennis courts, and a fenced-in off-leash dog zone. In the midst of it all stands Families in Nature, a once grassy swale that's been planted and curated to become a pocket oasis, sporting educational signage introducing passersby to basic ecological concepts and some of the avian visitors that frequent the park.

HUMBER BAY
BUTTERFLY HABITAT

Found on the northern edge of Humber Bay Park East, right where Mimico Creek pours itself into the waters of Lake Ontario, is the Humber Bay Butterfly Habitat. The result of three years of planning and construction efforts by roughly 750 volunteers, it was opened to the public on September 24, 2002, with the sole purpose of supporting Toronto's resident and migrant butterfly populations from egg to caterpillar, and pupa to butterfly.

On the southwest side of the park is the Shortgrass Prairie zone. This area is populated primarily by low-growing and drought-tolerant vegetation that frames the multi-use path spanning the park. Prairie smoke, common milkweed, penstemon, goldenrod, and various thistles and asters all grow with great vigour and abundance, providing habitat for clouded sulphurs, painted ladies, Baltimore checkerspots, monarchs, and other butterflies. On the eastern side of the path, behind the border of wildflowers and shrubs, lies the Humber Bay Shores Stormwater Management Facility, an assemblage of cells and basins used to

Above: Red-necked grebes on artificial breeding habitat in stormwater retention pond
Right: Swans in stormwater retention pond

collect stormwater and urban runoff and filter it on its way to Lake Ontario.

On the northern side of the park are the Wildflower Meadow and Tall Grass Prairie, a patchwork of grasslands, prairies, and meadows that constitute the largest zone at Humber Bay Butterfly Habitat. Here, trembling aspen and buttonbush grow to tempt swallowtails; chokecherry and swamp thistle service viceroys; and pussy willow and New Jersey tea nourish mourning cloaks. Scattered throughout you'll find cardinal flower, fox sedge, red osier dogwood, blue-eyed grass, swamp milkweed, and shasta daisy.

In between these two zones, you'll find the Home Garden, the Humber Bay Butterfly Habitat's most unusual feature and something truly unique in Toronto's

Above: Home Garden area
Left: Patio-style furnishings in Home Garden area

tapestry of green space. Here, visitors will find a semicircular arrangement of stone walls and flower beds that play host to a variety of native plant species such as butterfly milkweed, black-eyed Susan, wild bergamot, joe pye weed, and coneflowers, as well as several non-native ornamentals. These plants were selected not only for their attractiveness to butterflies and other pollinators, but also because they are well-suited to cultivate in the backyards of residential Toronto. Indeed, the very purpose of the Home Garden area is to inspire us all to rethink the landscaping we do around our homes and give consideration to stitching in

Red Admiral butterfly on Goldenrod

plants and landscape features that are not only beautiful to look at, but provide much-valued habitat for the countless creatures that crawl and swarm just outside our back doors.

Urbanization, industrialization, mass-scale agriculture, and myriad other by-products of human civilization have radically changed the landscape surrounding the densely populated areas of our world. Where once boundless stretches of habitat formed prolific ranges and migration corridors for our butterflies, today there stands something much closer to an archipelago, where isolated islands of habitat lay separated by tracts of land devoid of food and shelter. For many species of butterfly, the result of this massive transformation has been devastating. For migrating species, the gaps between acceptable habitat may spell the difference between life and death. For less mobile species, the isolation can serve to damage the genetic viability of the community. Whatever the impact, without our foresight and planning, the threat to these creatures cannot be overstated.

Our own backyards and public green space may well provide one of the best frontiers for conservation and remediation. By dedicating part of our own land to cultivating acceptable habitat, we can greatly reduce the strain on butterfly populations. A stand of milkweed and coneflowers can service passing monarchs, providing them with the hosts and nectar needed to fuel their monumental migration.

Above: Monarch butterfly on joe pye weed
Left: Trail near the park's Wildflower Meadow

Asters and dandelions can provide sustenance to passing orange sulphurs. A section of hollow log can offer refuge to an overwintering mourning cloak. A sassafras tree can entice the spicebush swallowtail. While some of these species may be common in Toronto, it is worth recalling that so too was the karner blue, a species once abundant in locations around the GTA. These butterflies were dependent on wild lupine, a plant that found its home in Toronto's few oak savannahs. As wild lupines faded from the landscape, the karner blue disappeared as well. Now classified as an extirpated species, it is hoped that renaturalization efforts and breeding programs will one day allow these butterflies to be reintroduced to the area, but the unique genetic stock of our own local population has likely been lost forever.

KING'S MILL PARK AND HUMBER MARSHES PARK

27

For thousands of years, the Humber River has played an integral role in the civilizations of southwestern Ontario. First Nations people carved an important portage route along its banks, connecting Lake Simcoe to Lake Ontario. This vital corridor, which historians have dubbed the Toronto Carrying-Place Trail, opened up seasonal hunting and foraging grounds and helped to create a network of trade routes connecting aboriginal peoples in the region with those as far away as the Atlantic Ocean. These activities gave rise to numerous villages and horticultural fields along the Humber, some supporting populations in the thousands.

French explorers arrived in the area in 1609 and immediately recognized the value of the Humber River and the Carrying-Place Trail. They established lucrative trade relations with the local aboriginal community, largely focussed on acquiring furs. Over time, inter-tribal conflicts and increased Dutch and British interests in the area ushered in decades of violence and strife up and down the Humber River.

By the end of the eighteenth century, the river stood as silent witness to

Above: Lower Humber Wetland near the Queensway
Left: Following the Humber under the Gardiner Expressway.

monumental change. In 1787, the British forged an agreement with the Mississaugas of the New Credit First Nation aimed at securing all the land from Etobicoke Creek to Ashbridge's Bay for the Crown. While the Toronto Purchase stood in dispute for almost a decade (with some details remaining so even in the twenty-first century), the British nonetheless began to lay the foundations for the Town of York in earnest in 1793. One of the strategic pillars of this new capital of Upper Canada was to establish Yonge Street, a robust route to lands far north and an important aspect of the town's defence and development. By 1796, construction of the road had advanced so much that the Carrying-Place Trail was largely abandoned, forever altering the value of the Humber to European settlers.

Obviously, lumber was a key ingredient in developing the town. With this in mind, eyes fell upon the lower Humber. In 1793, The British Crown established the King's Mill just north of the Humber Marshes. Little more than a shed housing a water-powered saw, it was nonetheless the city's first industrial site. While poorly built, the King's Mill did serve a demanding duty through the early years of the town's rise. By 1834, however, the Humber River powered a multitude of

172

*Above: Canada geese in the
Humber near King's Mill Park
Right: Bird egg washed up along
the banks of the Humber*

mills, and the King's Mill was retired.

South of the King's Mill, the Humber spread to marsh as it approached Lake Ontario. To the aboriginal communities of millennia past, these marshes were a proverbial banquet, a sustaining force for the peoples who called the surrounding black oak savannah home. The complex ecosystem fostered by the marshes provided a staple of fish, plants, eggs, and waterfowl that augmented the diet of corn, gourds, and beans grown in the village fields. The European settlers of York, however, had since grown to view the Humber as a place of industry and commerce. Raw resources were dragged to the doorsteps of the Humber's mills, emerging as finished materials destined for the town's consumption. Commercial fishermen now worked the area, stretching nets across the marsh to capitalize on the bounty of the river at a scale unlikely to have existed in centuries past. Over a period of less than a century, the ancient trails and fishing

Banks of the Humber near the Queensway

holes of the Lower Humber had been rendered obsolete as the river was adopted as a cog in the wheel of human industry and urban development.

Industry established itself throughout the fledgling city to the extent that, by the early twentieth century, the Lower Humber was once again poised for a new identity, this time inspired by the mind of a man named Robert Home Smith. Smith had purchased over one thousand hectares along the Humber, encompassing everything from Lake Ontario north to Eglinton Avenue, including the Humber Marsh and the former location of the King's Mill. Smith, a financier and real estate developer, imagined his lands as fertile grounds on which to birth a new and prosperous residential community, "a little bit of England far from England," as he put it. Smith is the one responsible for founding what we now call the Old Mill, first established at the outbreak of World War I as a tea garden and community parlour for his new Toronto suburb.

Only a few years after Smith opened his tea garden, the Lower Humber was plagued by a cacophony of swimmers, picnicking families, and Model T Fords. The surrounding residential community grew at an inspired rate, and the Old Mill continued to expand. Despite two world wars, the Great Depression, and the death of Smith himself in 1935, the Old Mill managed to cultivate a reputation as an elegant centre of culture and entertainment, and helped to foster recreational

Trail through the Humber Marsh

and residential development throughout the surrounding neighbourhoods.

On the evening of October 15, 1954, the Humber stood ready to be reborn yet again. Late that night, Hurricane Hazel assaulted Toronto with an utterly unexpected violence, and the wounds it left in its wake would permanently alter Toronto's relationship not only with the Humber, but with every watercourse that flows through the city.

Toronto was woefully unprepared for Hurricane Hazel. The city lacked meaningful experience dealing with hurricanes in the first place. Further, meteorologists had predicted the storm would steadily lose power after making landfall, and largely peter out once confronted with the Appalachians. As residents went to sleep that night, most believed that the remnants of the hurricane would bypass the city to the east, so they, along with the municipality, had done little to prepare for the storm. Tragically, their predictions were grossly incorrect.

No part of the city felt Hazel's wrath like the low-lying areas of the Humber. At over 900 square kilometres, the Humber River watershed is the largest of the major watersheds that touch upon the boundaries of Toronto. The waters of the Humber come from as far afield as the Niagara Escarpment and Oak Ridges Moraine, and benefit from the contributions of hundreds upon hundreds of streams, creeks, and tributaries along its course. Several days of rainfall in advance

View of the city from Humber River mouth

of the hurricane had filled the local water table to capacity, prompting the majority of Hazel's rainfall to flow overland through surrounding neighbourhoods and directly into the river. The water of the Humber River rose suddenly and dramatically to a level that was hardly imagined possible.

Residents awoke to the screams of their neighbours, some already forced to their rooftops, others stranded in the crooks of trees or clinging for dear life to whatever support they had managed to grasp when the flash floods swept them off their feet. Trees, cars, fences, even entire homes crashed their way through the raging flood waters, dragged towards the Humber, wreaking havoc all the way. Bridges tore loose from their foundations, set adrift rudderless in the swift flow of the river. Firefighters, emergency workers, and courageous citizens, desperate to help victims of the flood, found themselves powerless against the vicious waters, the flow so strong it would have capsized or destroyed whatever boats were at their disposal.

On October 16, dawn arose to illuminate a scene of cataclysmic destruction. Water levels near the site of the King's Mill were estimated to have risen almost eight metres during the storm. The floodplain of the Humber Marshes, greatly expanded over the years by the infilling of three of the original eight marshes, is said to have

Bridge carrying Bloor Street over King's Mill Park, south of the Old Mill

been submerged under a river some three or four times its usual width. As the waters retreated, a tangle of natural and man-made artifacts was revealed, dragged for countless kilometres from upstream before taking final rest in the marsh. Eight hundred militia troops combed the Humber in search of seventeen locals reported missing during the storm. Hundreds were left homeless. Homes and businesses up and down the river displayed extensive damage.

All told, eighty-one Torontonians perished at the hands of Hurricane Hazel, and thousands more lost their homes. An outpouring of aid arrived from all levels of government, as well as from the international community. Cleanup, however, was only the frontline of the hurricane's aftermath. Toronto had been delivered a brutal and unforgiving lesson: the ravines and rivers that bless our city are nature's domain.

Eight years prior to Hazel's arrival, the province had, under the *Conservation Authorities Act*, established a network of organizations meant to administer Toronto's watersheds. In 1957, four of these were amalgamated to form the Metro Toronto and Region Conservation Authority (MTRCA). The *Conservation Authorities Act* was amended so lands could be purchased or expropriated for conservation purposes, particularly those deemed essential to flood control and water management.

Start of Humber Marsh near south end of King's Mill

Thousands of hectares of land were acquired over the following decades, on which were built a multitude of dams, dykes, channels, and erosion-control projects. Construction within Toronto's floodplains was completely banned. Infrastructure planning processes and standards were modified to address potentials of extreme weather events.

So, it is in no small part that we owe Toronto's moniker "A City within a Park" to the impact of Hurricane Hazel. The lands acquired for flood control and water conservation, coupled with the parkland, tree canopy, and urban forests that flourish throughout Toronto, constitute an extensive and virtually unparalleled tapestry of greenspace now utterly intrinsic to our municipal identity. Government agencies, together with environmental organizations, stewardship groups, and passionate citizens, continue to work to expand, enhance, protect, and repair the amazing natural legacy for which we are now responsible. The quality of life in our city is, whether it is obvious or not, inexorably tied to the health and welfare of these natural spaces. While many might challenge how well we have attended to our duties year to year, few can contest that the momentum established in the 1950s and 1960s is still evident today, remaining a powerful force for conservation and restoration.

ECHO VALLEY PARK

Near the northwest corner of Burnhamthorpe Road and Kipling Avenue, opposite the Islington Golf Club, lies a small patch of green space pressed along the banks of Mimico Creek. A trail arcs in from the northern edge off Wingrove Hill, leading visitors down through seemingly typical parkland, with stands of staghorn sumac shadowed by white oak and elm. The park is frequented by snakes, ducks, owls, foxes, and Virginia opossum, not to mention legions of squirrels, raccoons, and eastern chipmunks. Native goldenrod and New England aster vie for space with invasive Chinese silvergrass and dog-strangling vine. Yet despite these commonplace trappings, the history of Echo Valley Park suggests a strange heritage, something unique in the city's tapestry of wilds.

A survey of the park conducted by the Toronto Field Naturalists (TFN) in September 1978 documents a peculiar cast of characters. Records identify an assortment of alien oddities including Chinese chestnut, Turkish hazelnut, Korean nut pine, European filbert, pecan, and Japanese walnut growing alongside more familiar species like butternut, persimmon, and black walnut. Henry chestnut and native chestnut were found lurking in the bush. Shagbark hickory and bitternut

House sparrow midair above a willow branch

hickory were spotted here as well. Heartnut, beechnut, hazelnut, and pawpaw all called the park their home. Few places, then or now, can claim to support such a diverse collection of fruit and nut trees as were recorded at Echo Valley Park at that time.

The unusual inventory identified by the TFN is the legacy of George Hebden Corsan, touted as "Canada's nut man." A runaway at age fourteen, Corsan found a living as a farmhand before entering study at the St. Louis Hygienic College of Physicians and Surgeons in Missouri. These combined experiences fuelled a fierce dedication to vegetarianism, a loyalty that lasted the remainder of his exceptionally long life. After departing the college, he returned to Toronto, where he became a fixture on Yonge Street, peddling fruits and vegetables from a street stall while dispensing sage advice on their benefits to human health.

Corsan invested considerable energy advocating for the cause of vegetarianism. He believed, most fanatically, that nuts were a cornerstone of great health and seriously undervalued in the dietary customs of early twentieth century North America. He wrote and lectured prolifically on the benefits of a nut-rich diet, and cultivated a reputation as a fiery and often controversial orator.

Around the time of World War I, Corsan purchased his acreage at Echo Valley,

Japanese Walnut

and began an experimental farm. Over the following decades, Corsan is said to have planted and cultivated hundreds and hundreds of varieties of nut trees on this property. He was responsible for extensive crossbreeding, hybridization, and grafting experiments, all in an attempt to produce nuts of exceptional character: large, soft, plump, and thin-shelled. He garnered particular attention from fellow nut growers for his efforts to hybridize Japanese heartnut with our own local butternut, as well as his crossbreeding experiments with various varieties of European filbert.

Corsan once remarked that spring floods prevented him from plowing the land, for fear of losing soil, mulch, and humus. That aside, the waters of Mimico Creek were, for the most part, a blessing to his enterprise, and likely one of the reasons he settled the land in the first place. The creek is the focal point of the Mimico Creek watershed, which lies pressed between the Etobicoke Creek watershed and that of the Humber River. At 7,700 hectares, it is the smallest watershed to breach Toronto proper, but certainly large enough to have kept the creek in a state sufficient to nurture his beloved nut trees.

Above: Mimico Creek
Left: Ducklings on the bank of Mimico Creek

The city of Etobicoke acquired Echo Valley Park in 1959, seven years after Corsan's death at the ripe old age of ninety-five. Surprisingly, it wasn't until a decade or so later that city staff began to fully appreciate the unusual makeup of these lands and make any attempt to protect and preserve them. The hikers, joggers, and cyclists who use the trails today are afforded little information on this remarkable ecological inventory, but this should not be seen as a failing but rather a mystery to be unravelled. Wander Echo Valley Park with a careful eye and who knows what you might discover.

ETOBICOKE VALLEY PARK ⓴⓽

The Etobicoke Creek watershed is fed by some 20,000 hectares of heavily urbanized land near the far western edge of the city of Toronto. Waters from city streets and natural tributaries make their way through residential and industrial lands, seeking out the sixty-one-kilometre-long depression that houses Etobicoke Creek.

North of the Queensway, Little Etobicoke Creek merges with Etobicoke Creek, the combined flow finishing the final leg of a journey to Lake Ontario that began up in the Oak Ridges Moraine. On the southern side of the Queensway, the creek quickly passes under the Queen Elizabeth Way (QEW) and into Etobicoke Valley Park, an idyllic strip of forested parkland of roughly twenty hectares that occupies the east bank of the creek.

Etobicoke Valley Park is a place of subtle charms and quiet demeanour. Along the creek, thin layers of shale lie exposed from countless years of erosion, juxtaposed against the blocky form of armour stone meant to prevent similar damage downstream. At the northern end is a baseball diamond, home to a hundred friendly games a summer. In the south, an old, decaying dam slowly forfeits its structure under a relentless flow of water. Near the access point off Horner Avenue,

Great blue heron in Etobicoke Creek

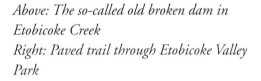

Above: The so-called old broken dam in Etobicoke Creek
Right: Paved trail through Etobicoke Valley Park

a small and sturdy playground brings simple joys to visiting children. Along the trail, an abundance of trees shade informative signs meant to educate those who stop about the most basic concepts of our natural world.

Across the city, there are parks that offer challenging trails to ride or hike, those that offer unique recreational opportunities, and yet others that grant access to rare and fascinating ecology, but Etobicoke Valley Park has little of this to offer. Instead, free from such meaningful distractions, visitors are left to focus on what are, perhaps, the greatest gifts our urban green spaces provide: escape from the hustle and bustle of city life, a blessing of moments, and an opportunity to strengthen the bonds of our personal, communal, and familial affections. What's unique about Etobicoke Valley Park is only what you bring with you.

FURTHER READING

BOOKS & BOOKLETS

Birds of Toronto. City of Toronto Biodiversity Series. City of Toronto (2012).

Bringing Nature Home. Douglas W. Tallamy (2013).

Bugs of Ontario. John Acorn (2004).

Butterflies of Toronto. City of Toronto Biodiversity Series. City of Toronto (2011).

Call Me True: A Biography of True Davidson. Eleanor Darke (1997).

Canada's Wealth of Natural Capital: Rouge National Park. Sara Wilson (2012).

The diary of Mrs. John Graves Simcoe, wife of the first lieutenant-governor of the province of Upper Canada, 1792–6. W. Briggs (1911).

Fishes of Toronto. City of Toronto Biodiversity Series. City of Toronto (2012).

A Fool in Paradise: An Artist's Early Life. Doris McCarthy (1994).

The Helliwell Diaries: The Diaries of William Helliwell from 1830 to 1890. City of Toronto Museum Services.

HTO: Toronto's Waters from Lake Iroquois to Lost Rivers to Low-flow Toilets. Edited by Wayne Reeves & Christina Palassio (2008).

Ice Ages, Recent and Ancient. A. P. Coleman (1926).

Imagined Futures and Unintended Consequences: An Environmental History of Toronto's Don River Valley. Jennifer Leigh Bonnell (Ph.D. diss., University of Toronto, 2010).

Lorimer Field Guide to 225 Ontario Birds. Jeffrey C. Domm (2012).

Mammals of Toronto. City of Toronto Biodiversity Series. City of Toronto (2012).

The Once and Future Great Lakes Country: An Ecological History. John L. Riley (2013).

Remembering the Don. Charles Sauriol (1981).

Reptiles and Amphibians of Toronto. City of Toronto Biodiversity Series. City of Toronto (2012).

The ROM Field Guide to Wildflowers of Ontario. Timothy Dickenson (2004).

Tales of the Don. Charles Sauriol (1984).

Todmorden Mills: A human and natural history. Louise Harzberg, Helen Juhola, Toronto Field Naturalists (1987).

Toronto of Old: Collections and Recollections Illustrative of the Early Settlement and Social Life. Henry Scadding (1873).

Trees of Ontario. Linda Kershaw (2001).

Unbuilt Toronto: A History of the City that Might Have Been. Mark Osbaldeston (2008).

Vascular Plants of Metropolitan Toronto, Second Edition. Diana Banville, Toronto Field Naturalists (1990).

Wildlife Reserves and Corridors in the Urban Environment. Adams, L. W., and L. E. Dove, National Institute for Urban Wildlife. Columbia, Maryland (1989).

ENVIRONMENTAL PUBLICATIONS AND REPORTS

City of Toronto natural heritage study — final report. City of Toronto, Toronto and Region Conservation Authority (2001).

Crothers Woods Natural Environment Trails. City of Toronto Parks, Forestry and Recreation (2013).

Don River Watershed: Report Card 2013. Toronto and Region Conservation (2013).

Don river watershed plan: beyond forty steps. Toronto and Region Conservation (2009).

Environmentally Significant Areas (ESAs) in the City of Toronto. North-South Environmental Inc. (2012).

Etobicoke Creek Watershed: Report Card 2013. Toronto and Region Conservation (2013).

Etobicoke and Mimico Creek Watersheds: Technical Update Report. Toronto and Region Conservation (2010).

Forty Steps to a New Don. Toronto and Region Conservation Authority (1994).

Glendon Greenhouse & Glendon Forest Restoration. Raised Trail Regenesis at York University (2012).

Glen Stewart Ravine Tree Issues Report. Urban Forest Innovations Inc. (2008).

Heritage Tree Protection Tools. Barbara Heidenreich, Ontario Heritage Tree Alliance.

Highland Creek Watershed: Report Card 2013. Toronto and Region Conservation (2013).

Humber River Watershed: Report Card 2013. Toronto and Region Conservation (2013).

Mimico Creek Watershed: Report Card 2013. Toronto and Region Conservation (2013).

Native Ferns, Grasses & Wildflowers. City of Toronto Urban Forestry.

Native Shrubs for Naturalization. City of Toronto Urban Forestry.

Native Trees for Naturalization. City of Toronto Urban Forestry.

Native Vines for Naturalization. City of Toronto Urban Forestry.

Natural Heritage Reference Manual for Natural Heritage Policies of the Provincial Policy Statement, 2005 (Second Edition). Ontario Ministry of Natural Resources (2010).

Identification of Potential Environmentally Significant Areas (ESAs) in the City of

Toronto. North-South Environmental, Inc. (2009).

Northern Nut Growers Association Report of the Proceedings at the Thirty-Eighth Annual Meeting. Northern Nut Growers Association (1947).

Protecting Warden Woods. The Taylor Massey Project (2008).

Review of Provincially Significant Wetlands in the City of Toronto. North-South Environmental Inc. (2009).

Rouge National Urban Park Concept. Parks Canada (2012).

Rouge River Watershed: Report Card 2013. Toronto and Region Conservation (2013).

State of the Watershed Report: Etobicoke and Mimico Creek. Watersheds Toronto and Region Conservation (1998).

Sustaining and expanding the urban forest: Toronto's strategic forest management plan. City of Toronto Parks, Forestry and Recreation, Urban Forestry (2013).

A time for bold steps: the Don watershed report card. The Don Watershed Regeneration Council (2000).

Toronto and Regional Watersheds: Report Card 2013. Toronto and Region Conservation (2013).

Todmorden Mills Environmental Baseline Study. James Kamstra (2003).

Todmorden Mills — Statement of Significance. City of Toronto Museum Services.

Toronto Field Naturalists' Ravine Survey Study No. Two: Brookbanks Ravine. Bruce Cruickshank, Bruce Parker (1974).

Toronto Field Naturalists' Ravine Survey Study No. Five: The Park Drive Ravine. Rosedale Dave Taylor, Paul Scrivener (1976).

Toronto Field Naturalists' Ravine Survey Study No. Seven: Taylor Creek — Woodbine Bridge Ravine. Linda Cardini, Helen Juhola (1977).

Toward the Ecological Restoration of South Etobicoke: Final Report. Environmental Planning & Policy Associates (1997).

PERIODICALS

Royal Ontario Museum Archaeological Newsletter Committee for Field Archaeology, Royal Ontario Museum Various issues (1990 – 2002).

Toronto Field Naturalist Newsletter. Various issues (2012 – 2014).

WEBSITES

CBC Digital Archives. www.cbc.ca/archives.

Citizens Concerned About the Future of the Etobicoke Waterfront. www.ccfew.org.

City of Toronto Parks, Forestry & Recreation. www1.toronto.ca/wps/portal/contentonly?vgnextoid=5b1619f8602a0410VgnVCM10000071d60f89RCRD.

Connect with the Creek. www.highlandcreekconnect.ca.

Friends of Cedarvale. friendsofcedarvale.tumblr.com.

Discover the Don. www.discoverthedon.ca.

Don Watcher. donwatcher.blogspot.ca.

Friends of the Don East. fode.ca.

Friends of the Spit. www.friendsofthespit.ca.

Friends of the Rouge. www.therouge.org.

Friends of the Rouge Watershed. www.frw.ca.

Heritage Toronto. heritagetoronto.org.

Inside Toronto. www.insidetoronto.com.

Lost River Walks. www.lostrivers.ca.

Oak Ridges Moraine Land Trust. www.oakridgesmoraine.org.

Ontario Heritage Trust. www.heritagetrust.on.ca.

Ontario Nature. www.ontarionature.org.

Ontario Trails Council. www.ontariotrails.on.ca.

Ontario Urban Forest Council. www.oufc.org.

The Nature Conservancy Blog. blog.nature.org.

Nature Conservancy Canada. www.natureconservancy.ca.

Rouge Park Alliance. www.rougepark.com.

Society for Ecological Restoration. www.ser.org.

Spacing Toronto. spacing.ca.

Toronto and Region Conservation Authority. www.trca.on.ca.

Toronto Environmental Alliance. www.torontoenvironment.org.

Toronto Field Naturalists. www.torontofieldnaturalists.org.

Toronto Wildlife. toronto-wildlife.com.

Toronto's Ravines & Urban Forests. ravines.to.

Vanishing Point. vanishingpoint.ca.

INDEX

REFERENCES IN BOLD REFER TO PHOTOS